The Collected Poems
of Larry Eigner

Larry Eißner   June 19 1970   #402
23 Bates Road
Swampscott, Mass.

                                     The imagined, returning
                                        what is
                                              endless song

The Collected Poems of Larry Eigner

Edited by Curtis Faville & Robert Grenier

Stanford University Press
Stanford California

Stanford University Press
Stanford, California

Printed in the United States of America.

Library of Congress Cataloging-in-Publication Data

Eigner, Larry, 1927-1996
 [Poems]
 The collected poems of Larry Eigner / edited by Curtis Faville & Robert Grenier.
   4 v.
 Poems.
 Includes bibliographical references and index.
 ISBN 978-0-8047-5090-5 (casebound : alk. paper)
 I. Faville, Curtis. II. Grenier, Robert. III. Title.
 PS3509.I47A6 2009
 811'.54--dc22
                               2009027644

The poems that were originally published in *readiness / enough / depends / on* (Green Integer, 2000), © by The Estate of Larry Eigner, are reprinted with the permission of Green Integer Books, www.greeninteger.com.

"Buffalo Bill's". Copyright 1923, 1951, © 1991 by the Trustees for the E.E. Cummings Trust. Copyright © 1976 by George James Firmage, from *Complete Poems 1904-1962* by E.E. Cummings, edited by George J. Firmage. Used by permission of Liveright Publishing Corporation.

Four poems from the typescript of Larry Eigner's *On My Eyes:* "the ragged lines of...," "If you weep, I think that...," "after all the singing faces, you...," and "every day afterwards I sat at the table with her..." from the Jonathan Williams papers are reprinted with the permission of Michael Basinski, Curator, the Poetry Collection of the University of Buffalo.

All writings and images that are © The Estate of Larry Eigner are reproduced with the permission of Richard M. Eigner, Executor of the Estate of Larry Eigner.

All of the poems in the Larry Eigner Collection at the University of Kansas are courtesy of Special Collections, Spencer Research Library, University of Kansas Libraries.

All of the poems located in the Larry Eigner Papers at Stanford University are courtesy of the Department of Special Collections and University Archives, Stanford University Libraries, M0902 Larry Eigner Papers.

The following poems appeared originally in *Poetry*: "Piercing the wall the window," "They would not rent or sell the," "The surgical waters," "Ply with chocolates," "Walls or clear fields," "much space along the," "stand on one foot," "The clock," "Where is an attic," "50 cars," File ("Let all those memories come flooding back"), "the baby cries he," "to make myself a world," "the water dripping," "the green garage door," empty the apartment ("blue lining of the kitchen"), "the earth you may as well," "newspaper circling," "blackbird/blue sky," "a penny/in the road," "The dark bird white bird," "the distances are shortened," "sliding down the," "the pipes how many," "the feet of Icarus," "the birds/risen to a tree," "summer and winter," "The wind-bell," "shadows, birds," "varieties of quiet," "Among various hills," "how/are things," "down there in the street," "the tree/roots water," "the strength of a wing," "dangerous," "the air," and "in the air." Reprinted with permission.

DEDICATION

for Beverly and Richard Eigner

CONTENTS

INTRODUCTION

Larry Eigner had great eyes—he could look *right through you*, or, alternatively, he could *look right at you* (or both, at the same time).

That very *presence* of the eyes—and the intelligence and sympathy and 'openness of understanding' in them—was what was initially absolutely engaging to me, when I first walked up to the door at 23 Bates Road in Swampscott, Massachusetts in January 1971 (Larry's workspace was the front porch)—this was determinative.

I was a creepy little magazine editor trying to crawl in there and get a poem (for nothing!) for my (unpublished) 'periodical' *this*—from the author of *From The Sustaining Air, On My Eyes* and *Another Time In Fragments*—and Larry welcomed me, warmly and openly. (This was his opportunity to *talk*...) His diminutive mother, Bessie, brought out a plate of snacks, and I was introduced to his father, Israel, who receded into the background of the house.

Because I couldn't understand *At All* what he was saying—in his barrage of (palsied) speech—he had not had 'opportunity to converse' for so long!—in my *panic* (after all, I knew something of his work and was currently teaching his poems in my Modern Poetry class at Tufts), I asked Larry to read aloud several poems which I 'knew in the book'—and thereby began the process of learning to hear what he was saying (because I could *see it on the page*, as he spoke).

I came out of there (after c. 2 1/2 hours, of that first interview) *utterly exhausted*—from the 'language problem' *and* trying to keep up with Larry's relentless ('monologue') energy and 'sidewise'/associational thinking. Afterward, I just sat in my car (the green Jeep, it would have been), before gathering myself to drive home to Lanesville, where Emily, Amy and I lived then.

It was immediately *clear* to me that Larry Eigner was a very considerable person, whose existence *shone forth from him* (how else say it?)—*and* who was one with a '*métier*' (just like, differently, W. C. Williams—writing—despite Stein's spiteful retort), a *measure*—a 'homegrown/American' *use of his typewriter* !

Did I emerge with a poem, for the first issue of our magazine, *this* ?

What emerged was a kind of onerous, 'medieval apprenticeship', in which I furthered his work with 'selfless devotion'—*typing it up* !—and in that process, coming to understand what *I* might do/what my life's energy might realize *different from/'out' from that* ! This edition is the 'result' of that apprenticeship, in part. (In former times, it was commonplace—how one learned and came to do the work, in a field—but nowadays, each new poet is supposed to be 'brand new' !)

For purposes of discussion—and to let Larry Eigner 'introduce himself'—here are six poems (from the over 3,070 which follow) which Robert Grenier would like to be able to *take with him* to that 'desert isle' (presuming he could not avoid going there, and that there was time to pack). They are short enough so as not to fill up too many pages here (we mean no 'discourtesy' to LE's many wonderful longer poems) and offer possibilities for commentary which may be of use to the reader encountering LE's work for the first time (as well as offering a *brief respite*, before heading off into the 'wilds' that stretch off ahead). Five of them are represented in the Selected Typescripts section in Volume IV, as well as in the regular chronological sequence, so that the reader is invited to experience them (now or later) in something 'like' the form of LE's original typescript, too. Spacing in all six, which we have labored to perfect elsewhere to mirror the typewriter grid, is only approximate here (for purposes of discussion in this introduction).

September 21 65　# e b '

```
flock of birds
        a moment
   of one tree reached

apples fall to the ground
```

What is most remarkable here is the 'literalness' of the narrative quality of this 'middle period' poem—it shows LE's extraordinary ability by this time to synchronize the progress of the writing itself with the actual occasion *progressing* (through the telling—and maybe previously observed event (?)), as these words 'set it forth' (in prose, one thinks of the 'long' football pass sequence in Kerouac's *Visions of Cody* as having such a knack for absolute 'literalness' of exposition of event presented, in (seeming) 'real time').

The "flock of birds" flies into "one tree"—"a moment" later "apples fall to the ground"—that second "moment" is taken up by blank space (ordinarily simply a 'stanza break') *enacting time it takes* for apples to reach the ground (one can almost hear them thudding, as the six syllables ('created' by 21 separately typed letters) 'fall' on the page), after the crows (?) have landed and begun to ravage the tree; it will be noted that the "apples" have now reached the "ground" (many *pecked*), and that the three lines above them *in the poem* have become the 'verbal equivalent', in space, of the same *apple tree*. This kind of literalness of exposition by the text adds enormously to the 'truth value' of what is being said.

Also to be noticed is what is *not* apparent in the poem—the usual omnipresence of the personality of the poet telling us this (often 'compellingly') and some kind of (often moral) 'directive' from the poet (e.g., Robert Frost), *telling us* why this poem and what it says are 'significant'/worth telling. Here there is not even an 'I'—the poem begins when something begins to happen and ends when that does.

This 'living-oneself-inside-a-Moment' and speaking from within that 'lived experience' is, of course, a primary value in what Larry Eigner might have learned from (Romanticism) Keats and Pater, but look how well it's actualized by the invention of this poem itself (see IV, 1704) and many others like it !

June 17 68　# 2 1 2

```
moon

   arithmetic
   in the night

rain
```

This would be a mere 'journal entry' were it not for the fact of the way *reading this poem* puts one in the circumstance being presented—i.e., doing arithmetic "in the night" (*inside*) wherein at first the moon is shining (*outside*) and afterwards (in the progress of the poem)—*after* one has been doing some arithmetic—in time, it rains.

The work of doing arithmetic (by, presumably, a human?) is one space 'inside' (and in immediate one-space-relation to) the shifting 'outside' conditions nonetheless represented by different/four-letter words. The preoccupied/continuing *work* (of a human?) is thus literally situated (by the spacing-structure of the poem) within a wider, ongoing event, of which it is a part.

Stepping back a little ways, it's like seeing 'him there', in the house, through the window, from the street (as in a Vermeer)—or from space—maybe even *writing a poem* (in an essay called "not / forever / serious" in *areas / lights / heights*, LE calls "language in verse…a math of everyday life") ? And certainly the moon/phases of the moon, etc., have had something to do with provoking mathematics.

Very 'condensed'/'simple'. In the Kansas typescript (see IV, 1708), this poem is centered on the 8 1/2 x 11" page (unusual for LE), using the whole page to frame/focus the image in its 'window'.

Seeing the words as composed of numbers (of letters) going about their business in/on the grid of the typewriter page.

                                        February 18 69   # 2 8 9

        the pastorale

          symphony

        the snow is
                  white   white

                in the yard

                  sunshine

                  the wind   sheep

              what do the clouds graze

                in safety as

                  a child feels

                  heedless

                    of indoors

              positioned   slow   like the aerial

            half blown down

                by the freak blizzard

```
        what this place may be

        unreally cold and wet

        when the music was conceived
```

This poem would require a *long time* (and *many* words) to explicate *properly*—perhaps it would be better (as I used to think, when I was a teenager) to say nothing at all (instead construct a 'signboard-of-myself', wearing a white glove, *pointing toward it*?)—Fine !   This is it.

"Pastor"—shepherd, hence "sheep". "unreally"—wow, is that a 'real word' ?

Imagine looking out the window (and into one's mind) while listening to Beethoven's 6th Symphony on February 18, 1969 during (and after) a "freak blizzard" and writing this poem—and all of these 'elements' are gathered together into one ongoing lifetime/lived moment on earth—all brought back suddenly/explicitly to inquire about the *origin* of (this poem and) the Pastorale Symphony in the strange (imaginary) conditions of being alive on earth "when the music [what is "music"?] was conceived" . . .

This poem demonstrates Larry Eigner's ability (by February 1969) to bring the imaginative *range* he had sought to develop earlier, in more ambitious 'excursions', *back into* articulation of a present occasion, *including* the imagination (music, etc.), as part of perception of the 'real world'.

This inclusion of a *lively*/'layered understanding' of what-is-going-on, in the poem, is a *boon*—a considerable *Stimulus* to being and staying alive. (*See* xerox of LE's typescript on IV, 1710.)

December 4 70   # 4 5 9

```
        a dark day

         all this time

          clouds

             birds in

               the air

                  and it rains

              trees

           a few leaves

                with

                stand
```

If it's a *value* to have been alive, and to record aspects of what has been 'true' in existence (despite apparent oncoming extinction of all species—eventually including the humans—and LE was very much aware (through Rachel Carson and others) of 'our predicament', was himself an outspoken 'ecologist' early on), then it might be a *virtue* to record the facts of one of those December days in New England, when it all just seems so "dark" very possibly <u>The</u> <u>World</u> <u>Is</u> <u>Coming</u> <u>To</u> <u>An</u> <u>End</u>, in 'miniature'.

Or, it's 'only' the particular record of *this Day*—December 4, 1970.

The *'timing'* of what is being said here—relative to its articulation, moving through the (available) space of the typewriter page—is absolute/'immaculate', so that what is 'said' (*on/in* that space) *happens*.

Therefore, "a few leaves" are still there—even now, as we speak. (Cf. LE typescript at IV, 1715.)

                                        May 3 71   # 4 9 9

        the music of

          the sea

        beyond

        the wood

          the wind blows

            the leaves

                they stay

            there   such times

          roots spread

            flower

            face   the sky

              sphere

              ah the seed

              not to choose

A 'prosperous', dreamy quality (perhaps best shown in 'dimestore' photo of LE on bio page of *Things Stirring / Together / Or Far Away*—a 'mistake' (?) shot of him 'blinking'/with his eyes shut, *but looking like* he was happily absorbed in whatever 'thought process' was then his good fortune to be wholly absorbed within!) governs this springtime revery (which is nonetheless grounded in the 'facts of the season', which give this poem its 'force').

The "wood" and "the sea" are at once literally the very familiar trees over there (between the house at 23 Bates Road and Massachusetts Bay) and some ('illumined') imaginary place (akin to Prospero's island in *The Tempest*) to which LE's imagination journeys and comes to know (and 'occupy') and articulate into possible experience for us, in this poem.

This very world is this magical place—where Earth's renewal (in springtime) *occurs* 'in real time', of the seasons, and all this *energy* (making root-branch-flower-seed) is *everywhere around us*, on this living planet, in springtime.

How should one "choose" (alive within the living fact of it all) '*one*' (rather than 'another') as a 'better exemplar' of this process (one thinks of Keats, who "cannot see what flowers are at my feet" in part because of their profusion) ? All round/about, it's a "sphere".

On page IV, 1716 below the reader may find a reproduction of a rare holograph 1st draft of this poem, followed on IV, 1717 by a (degraded *or improved*?) xerox of LE's typewritten (next?) draft; this latter object is possessed of *extraordinary 'beauty'* and '*force*', as a poem.

The word "seed" (especially as typed, in confirmation, toward left margin in LE's typescript) seems actually to 'seed itself' into existence—as if the word "seed" could actually honor and 'bring to pass' *what is* (and continue to 'operate' and '*grow*' into a next generation)—every (and any) poet might wish to develop the capacity to work within such "unexpected supply" !

"*calli + graphy*"—what is 'beautiful-writing' (in the eye of the beholder, certainly, but) it's not *only* 'the art of fine penmanship'—i.e., 'hand-writing', as in long-established Chinese and Japanese calligraphic practice—Larry Eigner's old Royal portable typewriter, with its *keyboard* (think Wanda Landowska and the harpsichord keyboard, upon which she performed Bach's *Well-Tempered Clavier*), has enabled him to make marks in space which *often* have exceptional written beauty, as such (not at all 'independent' of 'what the words say', but *as the means of saying it*)— one definition of 'beauty' is that 'it works' !

Larry Eigner was sufficiently 'exercised' by (and aware of) this connection that he wrote, in a marginal note to his poem # 1 1 1 7, beginning "calligraphy / typewriters" (see our various front cover dustjacket images made from LE's typescript of this poem), "maybe this would be a good title for a Collected Poems".

The typewriter, as a 'machine', made all possible—with the agency of the manual typewriter, one could range round (in the typewriter page—*if* one could type) with 'perfect freedom' (inside its grid—which could come to be a 'whole world') and capacity to *precisely* indicate exactly where each letter 'goes'—it's one 'answer' to Frost's prickly objection to 'free verse'—all that 'room for opportunity' and truth-telling ranging about inside the 'net' of the horizontal and vertical *grid* of the typewriter's instrumental capacity, making particular ('*various*'—one of LE's favorite words) marks in space—which register *both* how a poem sounds in time (LE had little opportunity to deliver his verse aloud, to a wide audience—when he did, persons typically heard only his palsied speech) *and* how it can be experienced also/primarily (?) as '*beautiful*'/exact letter-relations/marks in space—i.e., 'typewriter calligraphy' !

In his landmark, 1950 essay "Projective Verse", Charles Olson set forth the prospect of what he called "FIELD COMPOSITION" wherein a poet may take advantage of the precisions made possible by the typewriter to enter into an opening field of language objects, subject to varying forces, inside a dramatic arena/area where 'stuff happens' in the developing/whole space of the page. Following out from experiments in the work of Cummings, Pound and Williams, as well,

Larry Eigner's mature writing is perhaps the best (and most varied) fulfillment we have, to date, of tendencies and possibilities regarding the use of space in poetry gathered into and 'projected' out into the future of American poetry by Olson's theory of composition by field.

July 26f 90   # 1 6 9 0

```
footwork

 skateboard

  middle of the street

   between trees

    sunlight
```

This is a real 'moment' (evoking the appearance and vanishment of all such into and out of existence, and time)—but 'for the time-being', accomplishing itself inside an interwoven 'narrative-of-this-poem'—a very closely observed and 'animated-in-the-poem' skateboarder skateboarding down the middle of McGee Avenue in Berkeley—see how the trochaic accent emphases ("footwork"/"skateboard"/"middle") get balanced by that iamb "between", so as to evoke (for the reader) actual experience of two feet balancing on the board of that skateboarder (an interesting new word for LE)—and how would Larry Eigner *know that*, given his circumstance?—going down the middle of the poem (as if it *actually were* the "middle of the street")—all this in lines which (seem to) 'look like a skateboard' (now that I think about it!) moving forward steadily (one space at a time) rightward from the left margin.

In this poem, LE very deftly integrates the imagination (of how something might be done) with 'facts' (of what the eyes see) with language process (forming the occasion being typed into existence on the page): *one*—as if enabling anything to 'be', by writing it/testifying to it, were an ultimate value (*sotto voce*, without proclaiming this), as in Spinoza ("Being" is "the Good")—just letting whatever quietly *exist, through* these words (for you and me!) . . .

—Robert Grenier
Bolinas, CA
June 21, 2009

A NOTE ON THE TEXT

The poems in this edition were derived from three primary sources: Larry Eigner typescripts in the Larry Eigner Collection (call number MS 39) maintained in the Department of Special Collections, Kenneth Spencer Research Library, University of Kansas Libraries, University of Kansas, Lawrence, KS 66045-7616; Larry Eigner typescripts in the Larry Eigner Papers (collection number M0902) housed in the Department of Special Collections, Green Library, Stanford University Libraries, Stanford, CA 94305-6004; and the approximately 1,800 IBM Selectric typescripts of Larry Eigner poems produced by Robert Grenier over a period of many years, working in consultation with LE to arrive at authoritative, 'established texts' for purposes of magazine and book publication in Eigner's lifetime, and in contemplation of the prospect of the current occasion at some future time.

The Eigner Collection at Kansas was established in August 1965 through the agency of LE's cousin, Victorian scholar Edwin Eigner (then teaching at KU), who while visiting his relatives in Swampscott, Massachusetts had seen the state of LE's files on the porch (worn, dog-eared, disintegrating carbons and original typescripts in danger of being lost or destroyed by LE's own rough use) and providentially had the vision to propose the creation of a repository of LE materials in the Spencer Library. The arrangement, begun in 1965 and persisting well into the 1990's, was that LE (initially through his mother) would send original typescripts to Kansas and receive in return two photocopies for his own use. In this way the Eigner Collection was gradually built up (and eventually purchased by the University from the Eigner family for a modest sum).

The Eigner archive at Stanford (organized by Robert Grenier) is a gathering of materials existing in the house at 2338 McGee Avenue in Berkeley, California upon Larry Eigner's death in February 1996, principally consisting of xeroxes of typescripts sent to Kansas over the years (but also containing some later work from the 1990's not at Kansas), many of which bear marginal notes typed by LE on his personal copies after deposit of originals at Kansas.

A complete set of the 'established texts' of the c. 1,800 Eigner poems prepared by Robert Grenier in collaboration with LE exists in the Larry Eigner Papers at Stanford; a partial set (comprised of poems typed by c. 1982) exists in the Eigner Collection at Kansas.

As indicated in the Notes toward the end of Volume IV, texts of a very few of the poems contained herein, for which we could find no available LE typescript, are copied from the pages of the little magazines in which they occurred (and reproduce spacing, punctuation, etc., found therein, which may very well not have accorded with that in LE's (lost?) originals).

Our attempt to be as comprehensive and inclusive as possible in this edition was considerably aided by Irving P. Leif's *LARRY EIGNER: a bibliography of his works* (Metuchen, NJ: The Scarecrow Press, 1989), which tracks the history of LE's publications from 1952 through 1986 with reasonable completeness (though there must be items Irving Leif, as a collector of LE's work, was unable to procure). In the process of preparing poems for this edition, RG cross-checked all available LE typescripts against entries in the Leif bibliography and determined that we have included texts of all poems listed therein. What is missing?

As editors, our governing purpose throughout this edition of *The Collected Poems of Larry Eigner* has been to present (within the limits of our capacities and with the texts available to us) the whole arc of Eigner's poetic achievement—from his boyhood rhymes composed in 1937 when he was nine, to the 'spot on', stripped-down late work from 1995—in chronological format and in an equivalently spaced Courier computer font which preserves poems (as exactly as possible) as verbal objects in space composed by LE on his 1940 Royal manual typewriter—so that the *history* of LE's lifetime of work in the field of the typewriter page may set itself forth, in what is the best guess we can make of its actual order of composition, and come to be read and (variously) *known,* appreciated and appraised by contemporary readers and lovers of poetry, for the first time.

Regarding chronology, and our attempt to establish chronology, it is fortunate that LE began dating many of his poems from about 1959 forwards—and that, beginning with "# 1," dated June 29, 1966, he began a consistent practice of dating and consecutively numbering all of them (through the poem found in his typewriter, after his death, "# 1 7 7 7," dated "November 17, 1995"). Prior to 1959, the typescripts contain occasional dates, but we have had to rely on a series of indices contained in the sequence of the Stanford typescripts, which organize poems in accordance with an idiosyncratic system happily described by LE himself (in response to a request for such account given LE by Benjamin Friedlander, in the process of preparing his notes as editor of LE's *areas / lights / heights*):

A Note Detailing Tags

It must've been a couple or about three years after I started trying poems again from listening to Cid Corman's radio program and corresponding with him and Creeley et al. that I began labeling em so I could in short shrift record what I submitted where, but since I might best or could only pencil in a notebook lying in bed (nor cd I take a sheet out of book or binder to type on, insert it afterwards) I just figured to keep the labels as brief as I could for as long as possible, hence once I'd numbered verse pieces 1 through 99 I used tags, a, a1 through a9, b, b1...y9 then 1a...9z and then ab, ac and so on. I reserved AA, BB etc. for prose and had wariness, presence of mind not to go in for z7 for instance wch in penciling cd easily be the same as 27, but didn't think to avoid 2i through 9i, z1 through z9 and others. (I cdn't say when I first typed a record on a loose sheet—early on, it seems—nor since when I've done this regularly, sometimes penciling there, too. Not too bad an idea to have as much as possible in sight at once, no matter how reliable memory is, in a small space or on one page.) Also about as soon as an editor took anything I reused its tag, though never more than once or twice, seldom perhaps without adding an apostrophe, and later when I'd been 5 1/2 yrs putting more than one poem on a page (at first for a while copying a poem once or maybe sometimes twice over again below the initial typescript in triplicate or often as otherwise quadruplicate), for instance I had four different poems (ih/ih'/ij/ij') on one page, three on another (iw/w/iw') and, like, jm/jm'/ j''/j'm on another, sort of thing I carried on for at least 15 months ('65-'66), maybe any time space allowed, also I see now I repeated de within a month somehow or other and ab in 5 days (the four poems in early '62 and late '61 all writ I guess on the 6th floor of Massachusetts General Hospital but of course typed up at home). Kind of lucky I began dating things as a regular thing in October '59 after Don Allen sought for dates to things he took for *The New American Poetry* when he asked me to show him stuff and I did; before that I considered luck might more than likely run out, I might be jinxed and get writer's block if I dated, it'd be overconfidence, counting chickens before they hatched, laying claim to lasting fame, though one or two things I did date and besides I remember what I wrote in the Summers of '53 and '54 and (so too) "After 2 Years" in July, August, September or October of '56. en through ez or so are from '64, the f's and early e's from '63. From lack of recall and in some haste I on one occasion used xyz for instance and 101, 105-8 and 5L2 through 5L9 for things at some time after I wrote them, guessing at their chronological position or maybe to indicate I cdn't determine it. Some, like "Letter for Duncan," I never got to label, thinking their whereabouts would stay in my head. A few such aren't dated either, at least one of em likely anyway from before 10/59, likely as not.

Whew! So a good bit before June 15 '66, when I exploited kv, the system had in large part become chaotic. A week or so later I flew to San Francisco to stay with my brother [Richard] for two months, and he got me to start all over again with # 1 (June 25th), and with a few repeats (#913a, 913b, 913c and 913d could form a group or series, 984' I guess I was thinking might well be so-so by comparison with 984 directly above it) I last month (May '89) reached 1650.

This 'explanation' (in which Eigner is, in part, laughing at the complexities of his own methods of recordkeeping prior to June 25, 1966) actually makes sense (as one familiarizes oneself with the 'seeming jungle' of the early work) and was a crucial aid in our attempts to approximate a chronology and make an 'organic' sequence out of poems written before LE began regular dating of his typescripts. Chronology is *only* of interest insofar as it provides a guide toward ascertaining sequence-of-composition-in-the-life—and for those poems for which we have only been able to provide an approximate date (e.g., by likely year of composition), the series Larry Eigner sets forth here (i.e., ##1-99, ##a, a1-y9, ##1a-9z, ##ab-kv), which we have attempted to follow in the sections "Early Poems (1950-1958)" and "Swampscott (1958-1966)" below, has happily given us our means of ordering these materials.

We have, by design, departed from our chronological presentation by starting all poems longer than one page on a verso—so that, e.g., a reader could see and read a two-page poem on two facing pages, together—and also, as need be, in order to fit poems into available space, on succeeding pages, so that each poem may be *seen* and read within an adequate space for its realization of itself in space—while preserving, in general, the ongoing narrative of the life's work.

We chose the large, 8 1/2 x 11" inch page to replicate Larry Eigner's 'home page' (during his life)—the 'platform' into which all his great works 'went'/the typewriter page in use in the U.S. during his lifetime—we wanted a page *at least* big enough to present his whole-page-poems, *as* typed on his typewriter (he was very particular about where everything went), so that nothing would be unnecessarily divided; but in addition we wanted a design large enough to incorporate those last parts of poems, which LE often (running out of space on his lower-right page) typed back up on the lower-left side, so that (ideally) every poem that was written on one page might have that full page in this edition for its realization. (This was often, unfortunately, not the case during LE's lifetime, in situations where poems in books and magazines were made to fit into a predetermined format; LE's four handsome books published by James Weil's Elizabeth Press form one notable exception to this 'rough use'.)

Composition for Larry Eigner was frequently a free movement across the entire dimension of the page—he often literally 'ran out of space' when typing a poem which *drifted*, of necessity, beyond the nominal 'margins' of the paper. In an attempt to honor, insofar as possible, Eigner's developing concept of the page as a spatial canvas, we have challenged traditional margin placement in both dimensions. This has had the effect of sacrificing folios in cases where a poem's lines use space ordinarily devoted to a page number. It is, also, our wish that readers may entertain this eccentric formatting of text as an opening to novel interpretations, not just of

Eigner's work, but of the potentials of the use of a larger page as an expressive field of writing's experimental possibilities.

Larry Eigner considered himself a conservationist. What this meant in concrete terms, among other things, was a determination not to waste paper. It was Larry's habit often to *fill* a sheet with text, whether with a single (longer) poem, or with multiple, shorter poems—often dividing these with horizontal, broken dashes ("a line that may be cut"). The *holistic utility* of the page, both as a canvas (space) for expressive and perceptual content, and as a conservation of material (means), is a characteristic component of Eigner's aesthetic. Those wishing to explore this aspect of LE's writing 'ethic' are encouraged to study his typescripts, as these are the graphic evidence of his considered determinations of *where things happen/decisions are made*.

One might have wished for a larger typeface throughout—one as big as that in Larry's ('pica') 1940 manual Royal typewriter—*the better to see everything & everybody* !—and *also* to have been able to give each poem the *imagination of its own page* !—but then one would have had to have had the prospect of an edition, the number of whose pages approached infinity.

Regarding the whole occasion of our decision to replicate LE's typewriter spacing in this edition, see Curtis Faville's "The Text as an Image of Itself" (IV, xxvii below) and Robert Grenier's discussion of LE's use of his typewriter as a 'calligraphic medium' above, in re poem # 4 9 9.

ACKNOWLEGEMENTS

As we arrive toward the end of our seven-years' labor, Curtis Faville and Robert Grenier wish to honor and extend most heartfelt thanks to those persons whose care and assistance have *helped us* make this edition of *The Collected Poems of Larry Eigner* possible:

First of all, we must thank Richard and Beverly Eigner (who preserved Larry Eigner's existence, after his father died back in Massachusetts, and supported and sustained his move to Berkeley in 1978), for their *encouragement* to both of us, during these years, and more recently, for their funding of certain 'added features', crucial to the fulfillment of this work. And we thank Larry Eigner's younger brother, Joseph Eigner, for very kindly inventorying and supplying us with texts of Larry's first poems (with documentation of their publication histories).

Then there are the librarians (and curators within libraries, of Special Collections) who indefatigably *aided* both of us, in response to our needs: first must be credited Richard Clement, then (in 2004) Special Collections Librarian, Department of Special Collections, Kenneth Spencer Research Library, University of Kansas, who assisted Curtis Faville most amicably in his effort to photocopy the whole of the Kansas Eigner Collection, which forms the *primary* source of this edition. William McPheron, then (in 2006) Curator of British and American Literature, and Roberto Trujillo, Head, Department of Special Collections, Stanford University Library, were both a great help to Robert Grenier, in his attempt to track down and photocopy alternative/'original' Eigner typescripts in the Eigner Papers at Stanford. Kerry Livingston, Librarian of the Stinson Beach Library (in the Marin County Free Library system), *often* provided essential 'free technical assistance' in regard to 'computer mysteries' to Robert Grenier, for which he is thankful !

The following persons must also be gratefully recognized, for their efforts to help us try to find fugitive Eigner poems, as typescripts and in magazines: David Kessler, Staff, of the Bancroft Library, UC Berkeley; Melissa Waterworth, Curator of Archives and Special Collections at the Thomas J. Dodd Research Center of the University of Connecticut Libraries; Michael Basinski, Curator of The Poetry Collection, State University of New York at Buffalo; Rob Melton, Curator of the Archive for New Poetry at UC San Diego; the Staff of the Marjorie G. and Carl W. Stern Book Arts & Special Collections Center at the San Francisco Public Library; and Professor Benjamin Friedlander, of the University of Maine at Orono, who kindly searched his Eigner files but found only poems we already had.

As joint editors of the project, it was our task to supply Stanford University Press with, initially, a fully prepared Quark typeset file (a proprietary software program designed for use by professional typesetters) of the whole manuscript. Eventually, over the intervening years, as this software became obsolete, the task evolved into our supplying the Press, instead, with camera-ready copy. Merry Faville, a professional software engineer, was instrumental in installing and guiding our production of the complete Quark file, serving as official trouble-shooter in overcoming complexities and difficulties, providing solutions—both in the display software and with the printing gadgetry—to the special problems which the Eigner text presented. This project could never have been completed without her active participation. The editors' heartfelt gratitude is extended in recognition of her cheerful, selflessly donated expertise.

Susan Friedland worked with Robert Grenier to develop the Index of Titles and First Lines, and (often into the wee hours) researched materials on the Web pertinent to the Notes. Amy Grenier patiently entered the relevant page numbers (once these were identified) in said Index.

Curtis Faville purchased a first-rate light box, and Robert Grenier's neighbor, photographer & winemaker Sean Thackrey, sharpened and lent him his excellent paper-cutter, so that RG could lay out the whole 'home-made' edition from printouts of each poem (i.e., design each page & paste each up on 8 1/2 x 11" pieces of paper, for CF to use as a model, translating each page into 'computer-space', for future printout/reproduction here). Sean also taught RG how to scan pages of Larry Eigner's typescripts into digital format, leading eventually to the Selected Typescripts section in Volume IV—many continuing thanks to him !

Robert Grenier's close friend, Stephen Ratcliffe, often provided a sounding board and consultation about 'how to proceed'—e.g., in regard to drafts of Robert Grenier's section prefaces, and how to 'carry forward' an introduction (RG usually 'went his own way', anyway)—thanks, Steve !

We want to thank those persons who wrote letters of recommendation to the Stanford University Press 'way back when' (in 2004), supporting the prospect of this edition—especially Albert Gelpi, Robert Creeley (I wish I could embrace him!), Charles Bernstein, Bob Perelman and Lyn Hejinian—in furtherance of the idea of these books.

And we must enthusiastically acknowledge the informed/steady faith and guidance provided us by Norris Pope, our editor at the Stanford Press—he never gave up on us, but continued to encourage us to believe that we could complete the task, throughout our many years of labor—thank you !

Following Walt Whitman, we'd like to *thank* ('in advance') the readers of Larry Eigner's great poems '100 years hence' (presuming there will be 'opportunity' for such reading), in hopes that there *may* be enthusiastic supporters of the '*full occasion*' of LE's work *then*, like ourselves ! !

LARRY EIGNER CHRONOLOGY

June 20, 1893 – Father, Israel Eigner, born Boston, Massachusetts. Grew up in Haverhill, MA; B.A. Dartmouth College, 1916; attended Tuck School, Dartmouth, in Accounting; law degree from Northeastern U. in Boston; practised law briefly; began working for the IRS in the middle 1930's; retired in 1963.

May 30, 1900 – Mother, Bessie Polansky, born Slonim, Lithuania. Came to Salem, MA as an infant and grew up on Turner Street opposite House of Seven Gables. Attended Salem High School, where she was an excellent student, absorbing the culture of New England, so that its literature and history became an integral part of her family's life.

July 4, 1924 – Parents married, New York City

August 7, 1927 – Laurence Joel Eigner born, in Lynn, MA, at 11:13 PM, weighs 6 lb 1 oz; suffers brain damage from extended labor/head being squeezed by calipers (doctor said afterwards should have been Caesarean), with resulting permanent cerebral palsy. Lived for about three years in house on Pine Street in Lynn.

October 10, 1927 – Circumcision performed, approximately two months "late."

November 27, 1927 – Pid-yon ha-Ben ceremony, approximately three months "late."

May 6, 1928 – First tooth.

August 1928 – Begins crawling; doesn't get first 'walker' until age 11 or 12, at Massachusetts Hospital School (much of world thus tantalizingly beyond reach).

July 7, 1929 – Brother Richard Martin Eigner born Salem, MA.

March 3, 1930 – "Talks well enough to be understood, has good memory, knows a number of nursery rhymes, sits without back support, left side only slightly improved."

1930 – Family moves to upstairs flat in duplex at 23 Bates Road, Swampscott, MA (in tract owned/being developed by Grandfather Joseph Eigner), in area with many vacant lots & trees about two blocks from ocean (Massachusetts Bay)—one could hear the ocean from the house--& there was a woodsy path to beach; lived in same house (except for 2 1/2 years at Massachusetts Hospital School & summer camp etc.) with two younger brothers (initially), then only father & then mother until August 1978.

December 13, 1933 – Brother Joseph Eigner born Salem, MA.

1934-1938 – Receives home-schooling from Mother (who read to LE Longfellow, Eugene Field, Stevenson's *A Child's Garden of Verses*, Poe), and possibly other tutors; also receives Hebrew instruction. Has extensive physiotherapy at Children's Hospital, Boston, three times a week (w/ Mother driving Model A Ford into Boston & back). Spends part of two summers at Robin Hood's Barn, bucolic Vermont camp for the handicapped.

September 1937 – Poem "When All Sleep" published in children's magazine, *Child Life*.

February 1939-June 1941 – Studies & lives at Massachusetts Hospital School, Canton MA, completing grades 6, 7 & 8 (at school summers as well, with visits home).

c. 1939 – Gets first walker , "four swivel wheels and a seat in the back end of the frame" (LE in *areas/lights/heights*, p. 131) at Massachusetts Hospital School.

August 1940 – Bar Mitzvah, at home; given a Royal manual typewriter (rather than traditional pen and pencil set). Begins to teach himself to type, using right index finger.

March 1941 – Undergoes two cortex operations at Children's Hospital, "deep then deeper, exercises after or between them, the second especially taking hours..." (LE in *areas/lights/heights*, p. 130) in effort to help control movement in 'wild' left side.

June 1941 – Graduates from 8ᵗʰ grade at Massachusetts Hospital School, at top of his class; LE's first book, a chapbook of early verse (*Poems*) produced as printing class project.

Summer 1941 – Family moves to downstairs flat in duplex at 23 Bates Road (with more room for everyone); Larry and Richard share bedroom. LE gets first wheelchair upon return home from MHS, or not long after ("metal sides & footboards with folding-up fabric seat, one of the first such wheelchairs to be manufactured"—LE, *areas/lights/heights*, p. 131).

1941-1945 – Swampscott School District furnishes home tutors, so that LE can continue his education, in accordance with discharge note in his files at MHS: "Improved to attend high school"; poems appear in Swampscott High quarterly, *The Swampscotta*.

June 1945 – Graduates from Swampscott High School.

1945-1949 – Completes seven correspondence courses (including English (versification), Humanities and Psychology) from the University of Chicago, with Mother typing papers.

Fall 1948 – Brother Richard enrolls at Dartmouth, leaves household; brings e. e. cummings' *Collected Poems* home for LE on his first Winter vacation.

Late 1940's – LE discovers work of Robert Frost, Hart Crane.

December 1949 – Hears Cid Corman reading Yeats one Saturday night on radio program called "This Is Poetry" on FM station WMEX, Boston; begins correspondence with Corman which rekindles his interest in writing poetry, and through Corman comes into contact with & begins correspondence with Robert Creeley. Becomes aware of work of William Carlos Williams, Ezra Pound, Wallace Stevens, Charles Olson, Black Mountain group, etc.

Fall 1952 – Brother Joseph enrolls at Dartmouth, leaves home.

1952 – Goes to Brandeis University to hear William Carlos Williams read his poetry.

1953 – First 'mature' collection, *From The Sustaining Air* [10 poems] (Palma de Mallorca: The Divers Press), published and edited by Robert Creeley.

1953-1954 – Summers at a resort in the Catskills, Camp Jened (Hunter, NY), for physically handicapped children & young adults.

1958 – Book of poems, *LOOK AT THE PARK* (Swampscott, MA: privately printed; second edition published in 1968).

Summer 1959 – Richard Eigner takes LE to visit Charles Olson at Olson's flat, 28 Fort Square, Gloucester, MA; Olson immediately types poem by LE & declares LE's work to be "stone-cutting all the way."

Spring 1960 – Charles Olson & Jonathan Williams visit LE at 23 Bates Road.

1960 – Selection of poems typed up by Robert Duncan published in *The New American Poetry* (ed. Donald Allen, Grove Press). Work begins to appear with increasing frequency in a wide variety of little magazines, including *Poetry* (Chicago).

Good Friday 1960 – Hears Denise Levertov read in Harvard Yard, meets Robert Lowell & is introduced to Gordon Cairnie (proprietor of The Grolier Book Shop in Cambridge) by Charles Olson at Harvard Advocate building.

1960 – First large collection, *ON MY EYES*, published by Jonathan Williams (Highlands, NC: Jargon Press), with accompanying photographs by Harry Callahan.

September 1962 – "5 or 6 weeks after I turned 35" (LE, *areas/lights/heights*, p. 26), undergoes cryosurgery to thalamus to correct uncontrolled movements of 'wild' left side; operation helps significantly; left arm & leg thereafter partially numb.

1964 – First airplane flight, to St. Louis to visit brother Joseph & sister-in-law Janet Eigner.

1965 – Important long poem, *THE MUSIC, THE ROOMS*, a folded broadside, published (Albuquerque, NM: Desert Review Press).

1966 – Flies to visit Richard Eigner, now practising law in San Francisco, & stays for two months; stops over to see Joseph & Janet Eigner in St. Louis on return to Massachusetts.

1967 – *another time in fragments* (London: Fulcrum Press) published.

    – *SIX POEMS* (Portland: Wine Press) published.

    – *THE- / TOWARDS AUTUMN* (Los Angeles: Black Sparrow Press) published.

Summer 1968 – Second trip to San Francisco to visit brother Richard; meets Robert Duncan; goes to Golden Gate Park with Richard and Duncan during the 'summer of love'.

1968 – *air / the trees* (Los Angeles: Black Sparrow Press) published.

    – *The breath of once Live Things in the field with Poe* (Los Angeles: Black Sparrow Press) published.

    – *A LINE THAT MAY BE CUT* (London: Circle Press) published.

    – *Clouding* (Samuel Charters, n.p.) published.

1968 – Allen Ginsberg, Gregory Corso & others visit LE in Swampscott.

1969 – *Farther North* (Samuel Charters, n.p.) published.

– *Valleys / branches* (London: Big Venus) published.

– *FLAT AND ROUND* (New York: Pierrepont Press) published.

1970 – *A Bibliography of Works by Larry Eigner 1937-1969*, by Andrea Wyatt (Berkeley, CA: Oyez) published.

January 1971 – Meets Robert Grenier, then teaching LE's work in his Modern American Poetry class at Tufts University, who comes to Bates Road to ask LE to contribute to magazine he is co-editing (*This*), sees the state of LE's files & begins project of assisting LE by producing fair copies of LE's poems for magazine & book publication.

1972 – *Selected Poems* (Berkeley, CA: Oyez), ed. by Samuel Charters & Andrea Wyatt, published.

– *looks like / nothing / the shadow / through air* (Guildford, England: Circle Press) published.

– *words touching / ground under* (Belmont, MA: Hellric Publications) published.

– *WHAT YOU HEAR* (London: Edible Magazine) published.

1973 – Subject of "Getting It Together," documentary by Dutch filmmakers Leonard Henny & Jan Boon; Allen Ginsberg reads some of LE's poems in this film.

March 25, 1973 – First public reading, at Artist's Cooperative in Cambridge, MA, organized by George Grosbeck who taught at the University of Massachusetts, Salem.

1973 – *shape / shadow / elements / move* (Los Angeles: Black Sparrow Press) published.

1972-1974 – Visits Franconia College, Franconia, NH, where Robert Grenier taught, on three occasions to read poems & participate in class discussions of LE's work.

1974 – *THINGS STIRRING / TOGETHER / OR FAR AWAY* (Los Angeles: Black Sparrow Press) published.

– *ANYTHING / ON ITS SIDE* (New Rochelle, NY: Elizabeth Press) published.

1975 – *MY GOD / THE PROVERBIAL* (Kensington, CA: L Publications) published.

– *suddenly / it gets light / and dark in the street* (Winchester, England: Platform/Green Horse Press) published.

1976 – *th music variety* (Newton, MA: Roxbury Poetry Enterprises) published.

1977 – *THE WORLD AND ITS STREETS, PLACES* (Santa Barbara: Black Sparrow Press) published.

     – *watching / how or why* (New Rochelle, NY: Elizabeth Press) published.

March 19, 1978 – Father Israel Eigner dies. Becomes very difficult for Mother to care for LE at home, alone.

August 1978 – Undergoes neurological exam to assess health for move from Swampscott to northern California, where Richard & Beverly Eigner have ventured to provide for LE (Richard to be LE's legal conservator). Settles initially into group household for the handicapped in North Berkeley near UC campus, which proves unworkable.

1978 – *COUNTRY / HARBOR / QUIET / ACT / AROUND: Selected Prose*, ed. Barrett Watten (San Francisco: This Press) published.

     – *cloud, invisible air* (Rhinebeck, NY: Station Hill) published.

     – *HEAT SIMMERS / COLD / &* (Wall Writing/Orange Export Ltd., n.p.) published.

     – *Flagpole / Riding* (Alverstoke, England: Stingy Artist) published.

December 1979 – Moves into house at 2338 McGee Avenue in Berkeley purchased by Richard Eigner, shared by Robert Grenier & Kathleen Frumkin, who have agreed to be LE's 'providers' & to take care of LE (under contract with the State of California), which arrangement provides a home for all (including RG's daughter, Amy & KF's son, Ezra) for nearly 10 years. RG resumes/continues typescript project collaboration with LE, with intent to assemble material for further books & a collected poems (c. 1600 pages of 'established text' result); RG & KF bring LE with them out to many Bay Area poetry events, movies, gatherings of writers, etc. during this period, where LE talks with all & sundry.

1979 – *time / details / of a tree* (New Rochelle, NY: Elizabeth Press) published.

     – *lined up bulk senses* (Providence, RI: Burning Deck) published.

March 1983 – Flies to New York to read with Robert Grenier at the Poetry Project, St. Mark's Church-in-the-Bowery; holds workshop on his poetry, together with RG.

1983 – *WATERS / PLACES / A TIME*, selected & ed. by Robert Grenier (Santa Barbara: Black Sparrow Press), co-winner of San Francisco State Poetry Center Award (best book of poetry published in 1983).

1986 – Meets Jack Foley, Bay Area poet & host of poetry program on Berkeley FM station KPFA, who subsequently often visited LE & took him out & about to poetry events in Berkeley & San Francisco.

1989 – *areas / lights / heights: Writings 1954-1989*, ed. Benjamin Friedlander (New York: Roof Books) published.

     – *Larry Eigner: a bibliography of his works* by Irving P. Leif (Metuchen, NJ: The Scarecrow Press, Inc.) published.

October 1989 – 2338 McGee Avenue house arrangement ends; new caretakers move in with LE.

1991 – *A Count Of Some Things* (Oakland, CA: Score Publications) published.

January 23, 1993 – Mother Bessie Eigner dies in Swampscott.

1993 – At suggestion of Lyn Hejinian, show with readings in celebration of LE's life & work occurs at the University of California Art Museum, with LE poem beginning "Again dawn" displayed on exterior of museum façade.

August 1994 – Hour-long interview with LE & Jack Foley broadcast on KPFA radio in Berkeley.

1994 – *WINDOWS / WALLS / YARD / WAYS*, ed. & with introduction by Robert Grenier (Santa Rosa, CA: Black Sparrow Press) published.

November 1995 – Last public appearance as participant in tribute to Gertrude Stein, organized by Lyn Hejinian at New College of California in San Francisco.

February 3, 1996 – Larry Eigner dies at 68 of pneumonia at Alta Bates Hospital in Berkeley; burial service February 6, 1996 at hillside cemetery in Richmond, CA.

2000 – *readiness / enough / depends / on*, ed. & with afterword by Robert Grenier (Copenhagen & Los Angeles: Green Integer) published.

Fall 2009 – *The Collected Poems of Larry Eigner* (Stanford, CA: Stanford University Press), ed. by Curtis Faville and Robert Grenier, published in four volumes.

POEMS
(1941)

Founded in 1904 by act of the Massachusetts Legislature and opening its doors in December 1907, the Massachusetts Hospital School in the Blue Hills in Canton (15 miles south of Boston) admitted Laurence Joel Eigner at the age of "11 years, 5 months and 28 days" (according to MHS records, which would make it on February 5, 1939 (?)) and discharged him back to the care of his parents in Swampscott (some 10 miles north of Boston, on the North Shore of Massachusetts Bay), whence he had come, on June 29, 1941, upon his graduation from 8th grade, with the laconic/celebratory entry "improved to attend high school."

MHS was the particular brainchild of former Harvard Medical School Dean, Dr. Edward Bradford, Chief of Orthopedics at Children's Hospital, Boston, and was 'free-thinking' in its day because it extended the longstanding New England commitment to public education and development of all children (think Bronson Alcott) to youngsters with physical disabilities, who had formerly commonly often been 'castaways' (concealed somewhere 'inside', 'maintained' &/or infrequently alluded to), cripples etc., who died.

The contemporary mission statement at the MHS website (expanded to include many more persons than the 'student body' of 1939-41, which was then probably mostly in accord with those "youngsters with birth defects [e.g., cerebral palsy] and Polio" for which it was established) probably accurately reflects its purpose from the beginning: "The mission of The Massachusetts Hospital School (MHS) is to provide medical, habilitative, rehabilitive, recreational, educational and vocational services to children and young adults with multiple disabilities, assisting them to achieve their maximum level of independence in all aspects of life."

Larry Eigner *did that,* and more – in his 'field', he became one of the finest (and most formally innovative) poets of his time—and he also physically kept walking, in Berkeley holding on to a railing and drawing his wheelchair along behind him with his right leg in case he fell, until shortly before he died. He fed himself, ate with a spoon, got himself on and off the toilet, and into and out of bed, watched television and typed his poems on his manual Royal typewriter.

MHS must have been a big change for Larry (suddenly away from mother and father and brothers for an extended stretch, though he had been 'alone' at camp before)—and despite that it was a "rough-and-tumble" place by Richard Eigner's account (the family visiting Larry most Sundays, making the 50 mile roundtrip through Boston traffic to Canton, keeping in touch) where much emphasis was placed on 'physical therapy'/exercise of limbs and bones (think 'Orthopedics' in 1939)(Larry often recounted fact that they had him—'he who had lately crawled'—up on rollerskates, in the service of 'an Idea' !)—nonetheless (in combination with his mother Bessie's initiating/determining *hope* and *expectation*) MHS certainly must have pushed Larry Eigner to recognize/differentiate himself as a capable person, strive and communicate with other beings, 'apply' himself, *Exercise*, and in general *make something of himself* / DO SOMETHING.

We start with a facsimile presentation of Larry Eigner's *first book*, printed ('published', in an edition of 25 copies?) to coincide with 8th Grade graduation in June 1941 by his fellow students at MHS on a small hand press—*it must have been a Big Thing for him* (& them?) !

The poems are *entirely conventional* (but show a sort of 'mastery' by this 13-yr-old of verse form, and are *quirky*)—Larry said he once contemplated a 'career' writing Greeting Card Verse, and these might well have become that ('vocational training' *works*—SEE!) —and the printing style, complete with decorative initial capitals, lends a pleasingly antique look to each 'gem'.

How did it happen, then, that from these 'modest beginnings' all those strange/later/great poems 'flowed' ? —RG

Poems

by

Laurence Joel Eigner

This Book is the Result of a Class Project

of the

Eighth Grade

of the

Massachusetts Hospital School

September 1940   to   June 1941

Printed by

    Robert Blais

    Walter Carlucci

    Joseph Harrington

    Philip Smith

    Robert Wheaton

Illuminated by

    Philip Smith

    Laura Pina

    Rita Mikelonis

A Blind Man On Spring

THE hand of Nature plucks the
      strings
Of all the instruments of Spring,
And makes the wild echoes ring,
                    Of Spring.

And now I hear the joyous cry
Of all Birdland as they fly,
Northward through the cloudless sky,
                    Of Spring.

I hear Spring's winged heralds blare
The ringing notes of Spring's fanfare,
To swell the ever-swelling air,
                    Of Spring.

A robin in a near-by tree
About to raise a family,
Commences very happily,
                    To sing.

The ice-bound river now is free
And rushing by with sparkling glee,
It gushes forth a symphony,
                    Of Spring.

It winds through stately poplars tall,
To cascade down a waterfall,
And fill with sound the Concert Hall,
                    Of Spring.

Oh, it is wonderful I know
To hear a rushing river flow,
To hear the gentle winds that blow,
                    In Spring.

Nightfall

HE shadows of my
outstretched hand
Descend upon a drowsy
world.
I cause these shadows to expand,
I cause my curtains to unfurl.

Depart! oh great and burning sun!
You are dismissed from this domain,
For now the laboring day is done,
And rest and peace have come again.

Retreat into a mystic lake
And sink beyond a distant hill.
Depart! that mankind may partake
Of sleep.   And may the world be still.

Rain

HE air is as dry as the desert,
And the sun beats down on the
  plain.
The earth is suffering greatly
And feels the need of rain.

But look! On the eastern horizon
A raincloud can be seen,
And the great sun ducks behind it
As the rain comes down in a stream.

The workman pauses a moment.
A smile breaks through his lips.
The flowers open their petals
To drink the rain in sips.

Sunrise at the Farm

HE night is now departing,
The dawn is very nigh,
And now the morning's
   herald mounts
To the rafters, up so high.

The rooster on his lofty perch,
Begins to flap his wings,
Each day he almost wakes the dead,
So boist'rously he sings.

And so the farmyard is awake,
The sunrise to behold.
The cow is waiting to be milked,
The hen begins to scold.

The robin in a near-by tree,
Calls softly to his mate,
And presently they flutter down
To perch on the farmyard gate.

Schoolmates

E rise and dress in the morning,
We are greeted by the sun.
Proceeding to school we like to
    fool,
We have a lot of fun.

Oh, now it's time to get along.
We're on our way to school.
We like to play, an easy way
To learn the Golden Rule.

"We have been loitering around,
Perhaps we'd better run.
Oh gosh! I do remember now,
Our homework isn't done!"

And now at last we are dismissed.
Oh, we can hardly wait,
We have no fear, although we hear,
"To-morrow, don't be late!"

The First Independence Day

ERY slowly sank the sun,
  And a glorious day was
    done.
  The glowing embers of that
day
Have never ceased to cast their rays
Upon the hearths of lesser days.

The sun had left that day to be
A printed page of history,
Stamped upon the memory
Of all who love their liberty.
They had fought to make us free.
So let us keep Democracy.

Mosquitoes

buzzing of the wings
And numerous stings,
Is a treatment that I
receive.
And the terrible fights
With mosquito bites
Are such as one cannot believe.

The maddening jeers
Which come to my ears!
The mosquitoes are winning the fray.
They continue to bite,
I continue to fight,
For the rest of the unhappy day.

The Steam Shovel

HIS shovel roars,
This monster snores,
And at the sky it smirks.
It's always wheezing
And always sneezing
Whenever they put it to work.

You should see when it blows
What comes out of its nose,
A smoke that is just simply black!
But it digs up the ground
In spite of its sounds
And in spite of the smoke from its
  stack.

Finding Daylight

HE darkness falls.   The sun has
                set
            To end another day,
         But very soon the moon will rise
            To guide us on our way.

And now and then a threatening cloud
   Will blot the moon from sight;
But if we wait 'twill reappear
   To lead us through the Night.

And it will dimly light the path
   That we may see the way,
That we may once more feast our eyes
   Upon the light of Day.

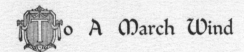

To A March Wind

Oh howl!   So cry!
And prowl!   And sigh!
And fiercely growl   And wonder why
And fail as before.   You cannot gain my door.

          *   *   *   *   *   *   *

Oh go!   You pout!
And blow!   And shout!
For all you know   And run about
Although it is no use.   Like a maniac let loose.

          *   *   *   *   *   *   *

Abate   Oh heed,
Your gait!   I plead.
Or meet your fate   The thing you need
Of you I have no fear.   Is rest. Return next year.

The Wall-Paper Machine

E hear a roar above us,
    That drowns the voice of all,
    They are making an awful
       racket
Tearing paper off the wall.

They are tearing off wall-paper
Where I lived two days ago,
Today the rooms are vacant,
And now we dwell below.

The constant roar of the monster
Renders deaf and dumb us all,
As it lets off excess power,
Tearing paper off the wall.

The Book

HEN a reader opens me,
he'll find
A thrilling tale to fill his
mind.
I take him very far away
To where the great adventures lay.

And when a reader opens me,
He sees the things he could not see.
He wears the boots of famous men,
And time means nothing to him then.

And there before his very eye,
The ages of the past go by.
And here I am for all to see
What power lies between my leaves.

FIRST
POEMS

(1937-1950)

23 Bates Road, Swampscott, Massachusetts (on the North Shore, some 10 miles north of Boston—*and* on the 'Atlantic Flyway', in Larry Eigner's early life and residence there, *when there were birds*!) is very near the Ocean (Massachusetts Bay)—Larry could *hear* it ('over there') mostly all the time, and there were 'Oceanic'/Airborne clouds, from the 'Great World' about us, unrolling in time, above the house, in rhythm with seasonal change ('Nor-easters'!)—and there were rocks, animals & plants ('*lit*' phenomena, surely!) ! ! (And always, also, 'town' life, too !)

By Richard Eigner's account (IV, xxxv), one went by trail a short distance through woods, from the house, and emerged at a sandy beach (Larry being carried by his father (?), a long time before light/strong Everest & Jennings wheelchairs, or his mother would push him in an old wicker carriage) and then they were '*there*'—and Larry (born with an extraordinary 'energy of person') could crawl about on the sand, and stop, put his head up, *look at the waves*, and 'cogitate'. . .

This business of crawling around, until age 11 or thereabouts (at the Hospital School, where he got his first 'walker'), had its advantages/must have been 'determinative'/'highly educational' in the sequence of how 'categories of apperception' get formed, in a human individual—for example, at the beach, crawling around w/ difficulty 'on all fours' (in part, dragging his 'wild' left side behind), one was a real animal/person actually there (with the sky/sand/water, and the other 'human' persons there)—all '*equal*' (none 'handicapped' or 'superior') in their (long-since combined and intertwined) '*there-thereness*', at the shore. 'One' was 'All' !   Remarkably, everybody/everything went on '*doing*' !

Thus '*evolved*' (by one highly speculative account!) Larry Eigner's phenomenal ability to think 'the local' together with 'the Cosmic', as '*the individual*'/'one' being addressed by the poem ! Why should any of us bother to (*compete to*) 'stand up' sooner than 'cousin Suzanne'—when further 'local'/'cosmic' understandings might be gained by crawling around for a bit longer ? (None of this could possibly 'de-emphasize' the *enormous* 'social' and 'operational' disadvantages and 'censure' LE had to face, as a boy born palsied in 1927!)

Kids can be really mean—if you're a little 'strange', somehow (e.g., if your nose is '*too long*' or '*too red*')—imagine what the 'total exclusion of company of other kids' (except for younger brothers Richard and Joseph) must have meant for Larry (he was providentially 'beyond' much of their commentary and censure—he was 'a cripple', really nothing more to say about him—*therefore* he could begin thinking (without impedence!), as an 'adult human being' *much sooner* than 'ordinary' kids his age (?)—he could set about his life's project of 'writing his poems' importantly into the *local* history of what was transmitted to him by his mother's education at Salem High School—and how 'significant' in those days (even into the 1950's) Longfellow, Hawthorne, Emerson, Thoreau and Dickinson *were*—all New Englanders!—when a poem (*valued* as such, for its own sake, as a 'poem') might come to matter to a citizen of any municipality who can '*read*' marks on a page . . .

These first poems come from Eigner family archives (and come before *and* after Larry's 1941 MHS booklet, *Poems*)—interesting that each (but one) was 'published' (why they were preserved?—Bessie's doing!)—so that (even without real hope (?)) Larry was 'defined' *by* his mother, *as* A Prodigy/A 'Poet' (think Paul Zukofsky), *invited to succeed, early on*—and he developed to Be and (with practice) Was One ! ! (He *is* One, now—"even dead", on the page.)

Initially, LE dictated these poems (as Richard Eigner reports, Larry would say " I have a poem!" (which he had composed in his head)—then his mother or father (?) would *write it down* and type it up). During his highschool years (1941-45), LE learned to master the manual Royal typewriter given him for his Bar-Mitzvah in August 1940, and thereafter typed his own poems ! —RG

Far away across the sea,
Is where I would like to be
Where once my fathers lived in peace
Near ancient countries, Rome and Greece.

I will dwell there too, some day
Contented at my work and play.
But now my heart, and not my eyes,
Looks upon that Paradise.

When All Sleep

When the sun is sinking
And the moon comes out,
All the little fairies
Go hopping all about

When the moon is shining
When in bed I stay;
All the fairies show themselves
And all at once they say,

"Let us dance together
And let us play a tune
Beneath the little twinkling stars
Beneath the silvery moon."

May 14, 1939

Mother's Day Present

Of all the pleasant times in May
Is set aside the fourteenth day,
When everyone has a chance to show,
His gratefulness the best he knows,
To his Mother, who from the very start,
Taught him wisdom from her heart.
Each has his own and separate way
Of greeting Mother on her day.
And though it may be somewhat rough,
I hope this poem is enough.

                    Larry

Great Grandma

Her mind, her body's fading now
  her life's so dim, so slow.
But when our children's children
  come to romp and play about,
The glow that lights our mother's face
  is wondrous to behold.
How all the ninety years between
  just seem to disappear.
 She's oh so young, so gay again
    Her Life's so new so bold.

Change In Our Town

The buttercups in our town,
Are as in Springs before.
And the wintry winds in our town,
Still pound upon the door.

But the birds fly high by our town,
They come by night and by day.
The birds roar low o'er our town,
The birds are on their way!

The lamps are low in our town,
The streets are wrapped in gloom.
The only lights in our town,
Are the stars and the pale, cold moon.

There are sleepless nights in our town
In factory and in mill.
The once long hours in our town,
Are growing shorter still.

We're working hard in our town.
We're working to procure
A new town, a better town,
A town awake--secure.

We've made mistakes in our town,
Mistakes that brought this night.
But another chance in our town
And we will set things right.

The Statue In The Harbor

The statue in the harbor was blind.
Her lamp was growing dimmer
And she didn't see the storm clouds breaking over there.
She didn't see the white hot flames that leapt
From burning towns and villages and farms,
And made the sky glow red with fire, and made
The land flow red with blood.
Nor did she see
The twisted, tortured faces of the men
Who burned alive amid the flaming, toppling walls
That were once their peaceful, comfortable homes,
In which they shared their sorrows and their joys,
Their work and play, with others of their families.
She only saw the smiling mask that hid the brutish face,
The silken glove that hid the iron hand.

The statue in the harbor was deaf.
She didn't hear the thunder.
Nor did she hear
The anguished cries of people trampled in the dust.
She only heard the explanations.
The reasons why the promises these people had received,
That their towns and villages and farms would go untouched,
  Were broken.
The reasons why the towns and villages and farms were burned!
The reasons why the citizens were trampled to the dust!
The reasons why!!!

The statue in the harbor was mute.
She couldn't speak of things she didn't see or hear.
She only spoke the words she uttered to express the dream
She'd dreamt.
Fine words were these.
And finer still the dream which prompted them.
The application of these words had made the dream come true.
But sometimes she forgot them and mistreated them.
And when the practice of those words
Was threatened and suppressed in other lands,
She went her way as if she, too, weren't threatened.
But the flames grew higher and the voices grew louder,
As the storm engulfed two continents.
And then, at last
She saw the gaping ruins and she heard the cries.

The statue in the harbor looks down from where she stands
And sees the dauntless people of those "conquered" continents.
And then she speaks the old familiar words,
But with a deeper meaning in them.
For now she knows that when this storm is spent and passed,
That she must never shut her eyes and ears and voice again.
That she must hold within her memory,
The simple lesson of this tragedy:
That if the liberties of any one group are threatened,
Then those of every group are threatened too.
And they must meet that threat
With deeds as well as words.

39

On Bunker Hill

There was a gentle hill with slopes ascending, near
A little town that bordered by the sea.
Where, in a silent hour, you could hear
The clocks record the progress of eternity.
It was upon an early Junelit night in Spring
Filled with the stars and with the starlit sky,
That strong willed men were on the march because
They had to fight if they would live as men.

A pale, low-hung moon marched with them as they went
Their dusty way, through woods, by stony hills.
Perhaps, as they passed by, a twig was bent;
And then the moon was silent and the stars were still.
At last, in coming to a quiet wooded place,
They halted and they gathered in the dark.
Around a light, they held their conference
And learned their destination and their goal.

And they could see the odds were heavy at a glance.
They knew the road was uphill, but they saw
It was the right way, so they took their chance.
They took the rough, hard way and gladly went to war.
And then it was they left the worn and beaten path
And crossed the thread of land to better ways.
A friend on horseback met them on their course
And traveled with them to their destiny.

(The only thing unchanged by time's exacting toll
Is change. Like water, what can it create
Unless it is directed toward a goal?
When changing for the better, we control our fate.)
And knowing this, they marched with destiny and stopped
Upon a hill and with them stopped the moon
As it had done four thousand years before
At Joshua's command on Gideon.

Upon the crest they dug their trenches in the night
And night befriended them against the foe.
They raised an earthern wall upon the height.
They heard the sentries pacing on the ships below.
The sun came up from over there behind the earth,
Still warm from its last visit yesterday.
It shone into the sky and turned it blue,
Then turned upon the earth and made it green.

With dawn they saw the tyrant sleeping in the bay
And in the town beyond, and he was grown
Into a giant now and who were they?
Then they remembered David and were not alone.
And they could see the ships at anchor on the sea.
The men of war, their sails filled with pride,
The foolish, boastful pride that makes one blind.
(Pride is but madness and the wise are meek.)

40

They were discovered in a very little while.
And soon the guns were trained and very soon
The cannon balls were racing up the mile
To scar the grassy hill that hid the waning moon.
The men upon the hill dug deeper in their trench
As time progressed amid the flying death.
They built a wooden platform on the wall
And mounted it at times to look abroad.

There was the enemy, there was the little town,
There were the cannon and the ships with guns,
There was the line of soldiers filing down
To waiting boats, their sabres flashing in the sun.
Here was a hill with apple orchards on the side
And pastures where the grass was tall and green,
Here clumps of daisies bloomed, for it was Spring,
And dandelions grew, for it was June.

The foe had landed and was starting up the slope.
They came and fired volleys in the air.
They shot their muskets not without the hope
That noise would frighten them and they would run like hares.
They came as on parade. "This is the enemy
Who comes and fires volleys to the sun.
They think that they are gallant--and they are!
But when has gallantry redeemed a wrong?"

They trampled on the field flowers and the grass.
They almost reached the top, but it was then
That each defender fired into the mass.
And some were killed but those that lived, attacked again.
And on the third time, when the holders' guns were spent
And victory was given to the foe,
They took the hill. "The day is ours," they said.
The day was theirs but drawing to a close.

The farmers lost their hill and scattered in defeat.
But when they lost, they won a victory
Because they made advancement in retreat
And left the mind of man filled with a memory.
Man will remember who it was that battled there
Against that enemy. He will recall
That they were just some farmers who were right--
He will remember and he will be free!

Candle

Silently rise, O Star
To meet the falling night,
Lend to the face of peace
A spirit light,
That, through the open air
Beyond the sun,
Dreams may be dropped from heaven,
And I catch one.

THE POLE BLUES

Slivers caught my knees, alas,
I crept on the piazza floor,
I crept in the bony yard,
but I wanted to get some more

I crept across the road
since I wanted to shinny a tree,
Once I got to the branches
    I should climb ingeniously

I crept down at the shore,
Stones between water and sand,
I started digging to China
  Right the middle of the land

Dirt under the grass,
my pants on the piazza floor,
I crept in the bony yard,
Though it won't go any more

Sonnet

Sometimes, at night, when I can hear the ocean,
After a hot and sultry summer's day,
It sweeps me with a smooth and mighty motion
Into a land of dreams, a phantom bay.
And landing there, I stand upon the beach.
Looking about me, I can see a light
On the horizon: far beyond my reach,
A star is falling towards it in the night.
The air is moistened by a drop of rain.
Here are no burning suns, no hot sands baking.
Within the confines of my little brain,
There seems to be a world of my own making.
I see a million stars and in my hand
I sift a thousand grains of moonlit sand.

The Comeback

There is a pear tree just outside the window,
Where, when the sharp winds soften and the sky turns blue,
The Spring comes up from the place that we thought was winter's;
Fresh and white and new.

For during autumn, dying leaves had fallen
Around its trunk, while the sky was growing grey.
And when the chill wind came, the mulch was forming
The Spring that is here today.

by February 14, 1948

Cloud Sculptures

Dim shapes in clouds that have no form,
Casting light shadows on the ground,
Move, as the winds that have no sound,
As if they had some destination.
Expressions of the wind they are, I know--
Shaped only when the days are bright and warm,
Yet somehow, when they come, and when they go,
I wonder if they have no hidden meaning.

Clouds that catch the evening light
From the setting sun,
Tell us some fantastic tale,
When our work is done.
Show us what the earth was like
When castle walls were high;
Then blend into a starry night
Of distant nebulae.

by January-February 1950

Noon

As I went down one morning, towards the sea
And met a sea-wind coming from the shore--
The ancient breath of life, that, with a roar
Like music in the heart, a mystery
Blew in my face and found an echo in me--

I thought of how, a million years before,
Inland the living came, on such a day
With such an air as this, to find a home;
And, in the hush, I sat among the sands
Wondering at the sameness of the sea.

EARLY
POEMS
(1950-1958)

So here was Larry Eigner—he had recently written (was it for 'Versification' correspondence course he took from University of Chicago?) a really *nice* poem ("Cloud Sculptures" on I, 44, mixing iambic and trochaic meters, rhyming very competently), and had stopped taking courses (though he testifies (in *areas / lights / heights)* that his mother Bessie would gladly have paid for him to take *All the courses in the Catalogue!*)—it was December 1949, he was 22 years old and (it must have seemed) 'living at home, permanently'—<u>What</u> <u>was</u> <u>he</u> to <u>DO</u> with <u>his</u> <u>Life</u> ? ?

Well, he *listened to the radio* (as I do, myself, even today!)—WMEX, one of the pioneer/embattled FM radio stations—one day in December, 1949, listened to host, Cid Corman's "This Is Poetry" show (as Richard Eigner details, IV, xxxvi)—and Larry Eigner 'summoned up the gumption' to write Corman (c/o WMEX?) a letter (*typed by him*, by now (?)) in which he took Corman to task for <u>not</u> reading Yeats in dramatic fashion (*as Yeats himself read*—as Pound must have 'learned first-hand,' by apprenticing himself to Yeats—*That's How Poetry Is Supposed To Sound* ! ?)—Corman (why? Why did he write back to Larry?) wrote back (encouraging Larry to read W.C. Williams), and connected LE with Robert Creeley (then tending pigeons in North Lisbon, New Hampshire—RC had his *own* radio show (himself reading poetry?) broadcast to a 'limited audience' from neighboring St. Johnsbury, Vermont)—WHY did Creeley write back (and encourage LE to read *Notes From The Underground, The White Goddess,* D. H. Lawrence, etc.) to Larry Eigner ? It must have been something about the way LE <u>wrote</u> what he said (?).

When you think of it, the 'literary landscape' in 1950 (dominated by established periodicals like *The Partisan Review* and *The Hudson Review*) was as-yet dismissive even of W.C. Williams (an 'anti-poetic' poet, in Karl Shapiro's phrase) despite support from Robert Lowell & others & (later) WCW's Library of Congress position--& Ezra Pound was in St. Elizabeth's (a 'traitor' in all but name, though he had been awarded the Bollingen Prize (for *The Pisan Cantos*) —in the 'shadow economy' of those poets represented in Donald Allen's *The New American Poetry, 1950-1960* (Charles Olson and Creeley, Denise Levertov and Robert Duncan, etc.), through direct communications initiated by him, himself, Larry Eigner (by virtue of his *poems*, themselves, & indefatigable letter-writing, presumably) quietly became 'one of them'—and he 'rides that current' (contributing his whole achievement 'after the fact', in this edition), 'even today' !

It was Robert Creeley's 'sponsorship' (and editorial labors toward existence) of Eigner's 'first real book' (*From The Sustaining Air*, The Divers Press, 1953), that made 'All the Difference' ! — and following out from that, it was the developing interest (in this 'underground' community of writing persons and their magazines) among Charles Olson, Robert Duncan, Denise Levertov and Jonathan Williams to 'collaborate' to select and make together Eigner's first substantial collection, *On My Eyes* (with photographs by Harry Callahan: Jargon Press, 1960).

In truth, in large part, it was these 'kids' from <u>around</u> <u>Boston</u> (100 years later, *in the 'same' place* as Hawthorne, Emerson, Thoreau)—e.g., Creeley was from West Acton, *next to Concord*, and went to Harvard as an undergraduate—where Olson had been a graduate student (from Worcester), studying under F.O. Matthiessen—and Eigner living in Swampscott (just down the road from the Customs House in Salem, where Hawthorne labored)—who have made a 'big difference' in how *many poets now* understand *how* a poem 'might be' ! Strange. ("The Hub")

One way of reading these poems is to track Larry Eigner trying to 'learn how to write' (bearing in mind what Larry *later* came able to do). 'Experimenting.' Some he labeled (in index accompanying Stanford tss) "a Dud." How *does* one 'get' from Stevenson's *A Child's Garden of Verses* to LE's late ('long') poem t h e r e ' s   a   s e a s o n (about the life of the Buddha)—or to the 'short' one presenting a skateboarder skateboarding down middle of McGee Avenue <u>as</u> <u>if</u> <u>it</u> <u>were</u> <u>happening</u>—'on-the-page' NOW ?—JUST WATCH (i.e., *read-and-see*) ! ! —RG

                    I
I can only play one note at a time
(and I've got ten fingers) This is the piano

and I should think of something I have to

                    play
and have to vary   without looking

   from   precision of simple things

bam

          with only that and
          the tune in my mind

              CARN

This car goes under the bridge
This car goes over
This car goes over the bridge
Where the houses rest
to where houses rest

Stop and romance is lost
Stop and ro-mance is lost
each car stops one place
each car stops in one place
But the illusion of speed
is keeping place

How nicely thy tents
How nicely thy tents
How beautiful thy empties
  How beautiful thy empties

The white lines by the plant
The plant by the white strips
The white strips by the plant
The towers by the lines

This car sees the bridge
This one sees the bridge
This car goes over the bridge

A W i n t e r e d R o a d

Rain and the cold had made the street
Clear, metallic; like a plate's
Stems, animals, and incident
Held abstract in one element --

Except this was all around,
Out the window, hedge, fence, ground,
Rough reality within
The supernatural discipline.

Maples stood unassuming then,
Frozen water budding them,
Bud piled on bud   each opening
Awake to this fierce whitening.

Tall grass, weighed over, matted, lined,
Was tangled in a quick design
And a stringent thatch of frost
Which let no spore, no seed be lost.

Only the houses and telephone poles
Were ample, wooden, free, almost
Their spring, fall, summer selves. Slack wires
Spaced windless air with their firm layer

And outdoor cripples, elbow-oared
In the road lurched slowly homeward, towards
Where they could witness this alone
And ring up neighbors on the phone.

"Keep at it," they say when they see L.
reading, then disappear down the front steps
 and plenty die, playing the black market
  a heart attack in middle age

        L a r g e

I tried to put them together
As contrast Beauties are
houses and the flat sun

Fallen in admiration
World of
      the mind

for how is joy forever
not continual Rain
and trees
      star gutteral ponds

            Impact increases

And still they become familiar

          elsewhere the flood started

             D a y   C r o w d   W e a t h e r

Life by eating and passing
solid and water
 parts are constantly changed
every two springs
        different man

     How much bigger, for a while bigger

        Fall leaves
alternate
Winter and summer, familiar
          two main seasons

But scarcely enough
This tree grown for
the phone wires
              airy space
between the upright branches and the lower ones
it is scanty and rich too

when I see the branches which yet twist like trails
ride and making room
 and yet still standing after all

the sprays that survive me

         Heat came
early for some reason
though first it was hot and then it was cold
excitement, and exhaustion, then fog
like mugginess, out of sight but
soaking, then a strong wind
from the south, mind you, which was damp besides
and slammed doors
                      In the
street quiet like safe buildings an
Africa with rose-bushes and lilies even
 flashing color,while above half the opposite
wind
bearing down
an autumn tunnel roaring

On the same day. Each forest
robins at some recesses
shouting or
holding with joy to
rollicking ground

        the flat islands float up high

          sun beating through wind
the eyes their elements

Starting the place was foreign
     still chilly with sleep, what would be
     hottest

                the time when Romans were at school
and then two children,walked
and schoolbusses for some stretch
            we were so fast
surprised, the clock seemed absent

Lately
        the usual daytime
at last

        now, again

go back, slouch
                    found
                different position
                                all of a sudden

                and feet
under or
 lying that way

scene, it might have been magic
roadbed cut dream
this speed not impossible with
wind in the ear, the nostril fan

   down the car pulling you,you forward
the car sling out at the corner

        the abstract forces

            hitherto abstract

Lower and the sky's acts
    which somehow is forgotten
 something against something
not seen
            suggesting all possible continents

that supple country
                        always
        forgotten
                wasteless

clouds marks currents each way

Random panes about the dark
 the doorknob,   low frieze
the room familiar as it was
yes, there it is again, the picture
as if I could feel my way
the sun always shining directly

back as we try, also, for sleep
and then we cannot go on watching, forever

This I have never dreamed
  (as if that would do anything

and the pants will stand out, down from the chair
      in the different light
and the bureau, choir, opposing the hollow

As music is the air
Devising time with gay bows
And trees in their places move,
The summer is going

Objects and spaces
Disrupt the mind because
Fast, the world isn't furniture

Winter is fiery and dismal
Our skins are not yet against it
  but the mind is delightful

            F e s t e

The children were frightened by crescendoes
cars coming fowards in the movies

That is,before they found out love,
that is, Comedy

        the cheeks blew
  music rises and continues

and the sea does

and there were no accidents today
the bombs showered us in the air

A flat-faced dog
with his nose on the ground--
that's my contention

    fooling any bone
    the unskilled hand
    rolling it
    one way and another

    the eyes crossing
    then taking it angrily
    a champ between the teeth

or a horse with blinders
tossing cannot
grasp what's behind

everything became nothing
I could not sit still

travelled and saw a thing
close and it disappeared

Almost, I think
I got inside of it

Now the autumn sun
everywhere makes me sleepy

September 51

to break up time, as it goes on, and
reorganize, cast back
on memory, may be
coming and going,
even when what is spawned
is death, the blind of an alley
    or the end of a twig

It comes to end, then, and coming
and going goes on. But
sound, another matter,
involves no reflection, crosses no doors
comes forward

However, when
we turn our heads for a minute
 this time has gotten away .

One of a Series

The tray his best friend started him wriggling
all of a sudden; at which reclused he read;
after ten years; down went his head
further in a clinch. Shoulder or fingers
fixed in an act forever very nagging
unless he could forget a certain way
what he was up to and how useless it was
in a certain sense remember and be mad

himselfhimself, his limbs and his mind
and so much sooner his tract, but he couldn't help that:
often as not he must live excitedly
and what happened to others would finally happen to him
--which self was wild now? A waste Well, he
laid it aside and held the book in his lap.

c. 1950-52   # 1 2

no chair tipped over

C h e r r y   O r c h a r d

The stage, a former playroom
had sunny, afternoon windows
in a white past,
budding and childish
 and doors busy
                  things,taking their places
people laughing and stalling

   as they finally had to move

   An old man lying down

       My grandfather emigrated
       the same day

others achieving

control of every thing

the stage is black and white

The stage looms forward.
minus the slave, the orchard
      the noble kitchen
    -canaries

Distance from Concord

The constitution one of a mass
facing Bunker Hill
   over the new bridge
Behind the sea sparkling at
morning or night the sea
Beside it airstrips
A toehold

    on this bridge you don't stop

Crane:

Man chasing the sky, or the hills
surrounding, or the other figure
he loped through the battle, finding courage
It was because of
                luck he survived
and went back to the lively woods

        Company

He saw things without thinking they
didn't let him look, they
included him

so much That his eyes hung like moss

they were vivid Surprising
time locked in the air
 like startling type
He came through and
killed a few himself

55

F o r e w o r d

The motion appearing the plan will become
definite, as a tree, with different ways,
so many pores, not a wall
angles or shelves with
inscrutables hidden, but
not covered
                a roof moving in fragments, then,
impenetrable ceiling, something at last
behind any tangible
                    bark
so different from a mirror's back

or, as some say, women's eyes
Or, where does skin come from?
the weaving of fish in half-light

Frankly, the best we can grasp is half
(Make possibilities out of time)

  Take true conventions: how are they made?

I n t h i s c a s e

Two quick explosions of the body
    cause of irruption of blood
as if a signal for a gun
but everything was as before

Cross country trying to save yourself
   asleep you don't know   Cross country
 to kill a summer and
  climb mountains
     watch the bays

   Milestone, a cardinal in a red hat
 shooting grouse, an old man
   ploughing

        mass of night, stars off the dark
                autumn is awake

        life being unnecessary

     Without life, death would be nothing

          T h i s

the weather surrounding us, even blue
from our nostrils   even
walls of storm, soft or
                        horizontal sea

scape, height above which can't be reached
the abstract ceiling, the sky   Think it petty
 the way it is   think
excuse riding life like a horse
up and down   up and down   or
a car is it
              but go inside
see it, looking outward

   the room is like a nursery
a seagull of certain definite loci
makes backgrounds, dazzles and sleeps
at one time   induces sleep

A book on my knees, my sensitive reflex
A gull, diving, looked like a plane, and scared me

                  but just enough
yet allow the air into your heads

        Such different surfaces prevent
distraction   stop in the end
contemplation   neutral room

Still the weather changes O
be the same
            day and night
blocks the window and the sea

  what to expect
                these
                    things
                           ex
                            pect

         in the blackout
   waiting for death, wanting sleep
   and the walls had nothing more to reflect

         world
                  the sea
   a shock wave
    and fliers a mile away
   were planes of another country

   Afterwards the sun came around

   and they say how
   stars will collide

      S t a t u a r y

   Graduates always smile
   in the ads for Switzerland
   bombers fly
   over the game

              heart
                city

   gods
   everywhere
   have shrines in narrow places

   and the V-parade
    worships the gone

   Hod-carriers come in cars
   to serve, slow time
   centuries build
   surveyed houses
   slimmer than tudor

   On the other side a
   crisis is reported,
   paradoxical
   situation
   that hasn't yet arrived

   You can read it backwards
   through set beginnings

   A likely thing
   there's no end.

                H

In one point: split. We were.
No pins. Not here, not there,
but everywhere, at once.
                         We think
it was, perhaps, the best way.
We phoenixes, unliable to rise again

I do so little

because the drive

of the world

is so much

It meets me, going

        the other way

through me

And when there is silence

all naked. I sit here

trying to hold my breath

but sometimes

in the livingroom

the wind

is felt

shaking

the house

Now I put her away, combustible beauty
with ideas of little use

    what did those goings-on amount to
at night   Was she there
Was she there, always?

             hair and brown eyes
which I can hardly remember

 and the bent moments of her face
 I only saw glimpses of

        and have her mixed up with
others from history

Before there were planes I don't think
the clouds looked solid now
I know that
but shadings, and above
light nacelles, V-heads, stones
riding at the sides of their wings
which sweep forewards, their own shapes

map of gyros and screws
explode someday
dreadnaught

I like to skim
push the cape in
around me a plane
 unseen
or a legless cat
attaching from its back

but that complete power breaks off
changing its course an inch

after nothing in the sky

              F o r   t h e   W i n d s

Put together
                    carved
   the violin

lower parts, or

the oboe
   over the hill -

top in the strengthening tone

   and protracted stamp
     then
                    not wood

             L e   M a r c h a n d

  Let there be pretended trouble
                             Portia's mad
    dress as a boy
                  to tell tall stories
       after marriage
                    to be on the spot
                               to the end

  but then to bed
  How would she sleep in those inns
  "Courted"by strange men
                     became vital
                               by a trick

  the Jew converted
                    no more gripes
  so shines a good deed but
  the Jewess well schooled
                     in the nature of Thisbe
       a little shrewed
       the nice man taught her
                       Plato's myth

  of Shylock no more but
                    what did his friend say

       the importance of sincerity?

Romance

to enter another man

        though himself
        in his own place far
        more than anywhere
        a man must stand,
        no snake is there

To feel other space
than what you are

        deliberate steps
        distinct if man
        should lose like wind
        he doesn't come
        like lightning again

Then, where are you? You
reduce to unreal skin

        I, knowing
        members and having flapped
        elbows, imagine wings,
        outlines, not tooled hands,
        at distance, partly by eye
        slightly round and up
        holding my lap

c. 1952   # 2 6

Mock Wagner's

Broken conventions matter
good Orchestration
sound like air between
viewers and the play behind it

heroic tunics flats
deep, deep, and serious

        but somebody laughs at last

              P a r t s   o f   S a l e m

                          down to the folds
I saw the upper halves of cars
without the wheels I know to be
moving around my corner, and
the action of those sitting there still
forward, drivers and children,   hands
a new hat on an old man
the street sudden smile at noise

last among the marble sites
and the brick exchanges
                          rises of earth
filled and massed with human stone
parking space alleviates
ancient commons which were lonely
and magnificent prairies breaking the heart

  because it was five yards off
talkers at one curb   lost as
if forgotten   yet
what has there been, now, to speak of

Girls and mothers of one hour
in passing in tender hair
and men counting silently

                                        c. 1951-52

        T h e   D a r i n g   Y o u n g   M a n
            o n   H i s   B a c k

It's all a waste of time: pain is
And satisfaction's preferable
But let me on that level spend it freely

On the high plane why should boredom develop?
It's happened many times. I should know better
Enjoy nothing, the absence of trouble

Somethere is there, but only unexpected
Nothing was useless
                    that I can remember
I do as I please, going from here to there

  (The farther I go, the better it may be.

O c c a s i o n a l l y

Well, they're used to it
 in those days we
didn't have floors
like now, no
electricity no telephone
radio no vacuum
cleaner But don't you think it's too bad
that college isn't nearer home?
You could get bread for five cents
I came here no faucets
a pump in the yard

Grandma raised a family
one room over there
                        The Two Old Men
born in one bed

            What are you talking about

Eskimoes, even they who remember
slightly better times?
                        while they live
they barely balanced their land

No consequence
                Remember now

ALL I CAN ADD IS
from where the war is
and more hardship

you'd be surprised

  said grandmother
                        after seventy years
    after a hundred years

c. 1952

        N o r t h

   the leaves headed green
already in mouth surfaces
                          I can't see reflect
the sun from where the sunlight strikes
all of color/ the
spots are indefinite; but
the parts alter

  there is always a sun to some leaf

    and as well shadow is everywhere
the sun alters a
vivid and light spray
shot half a block from an already
dark hill

    there are all kinds of leaves and
as before there was not one
they do not space themselves

          we have the moon which rises
  soon enough

and variously.
the sun having a long ray
one by one   and 4 corners
eight misshapen corners
and sixteen hiding behind
the leaves
          is still
          far from the spiders

RETURN FROM NOTHING
ARTICULATION
A WORLD

 For a long time
 I had not
 looked at the sky

  and there
  were infinite
  clouds, a real map

 among the houses
 along blue
 paths,moving but
      overhead
 which they harbored

 and branches from nowhere
 going up into it

      Some Numbers

Down by various ways   different men
but would like to travel
              one man

  Multiple fingers, drubbing, MULTIPLE FINGERS

the hornet, making his
flighty
     wave the air

in the eye, the eye
Be there, be there
many streets
       down outside walls

but not passing

Would like to see
a plane crash, something
excitement, plane
fast, upright, faster
than light, where
the mind can't go

          vertical

or settle
the alert body
the eyes
on stone
placed in earth
sky mountains
chimneys
 billboards

What's to be done
about it, peace
the whole lake
               in technicolor

past pioneers,
these little things
reminders that Indians were People

        once a revelation

And eastward, elsewhere, the same day
two dead migs   as I heard
                    like flies

fingers and toes whisper
the grass

nearby

the roller-coaster is

S u n d a y

You look only in one direction
or on one side

But the city is around us
like the giant words taking so much space

streets at little angles
alleys, dividing the block
in the corner of the routes

down which the stories at once rise

        driven by rain, the birds sing,
        elongated recess, deadend square
        looked over by substantial houses
        which were fashionable, now more quiet

        the tree growing as if outdoors

the curbing a shore they cross
cartracks and increasing traffic
to the pleasantly far walk
local varieties, the home of chocolates
welcome chancel-lots of garage
behind
modern slicks of industry

   thousands of squares
the footbridge brace the great river
the famous field famous
for hit runs.
                four hundred feet
is the equal of apartments
curving hospitals between
their older restful wings
Sometimes a foul reaches that height

        straight from nothing rain
        hurrying company!
        for one moment drawing shape
        the attic's infinitessimal distance

a single girl against the
clothing-store's wall

 new by the front windows
in the out-of-the-way familiar suburb
half in sight of the bridge,

passes you rise
in like chutes viewing the street
then only paving   then
the clotheslines of slums
before whole zones, yet
you're not in them,
 lanes meeting the deck in the air

                    you only look
at them

         above gastanks wharves railroads

                 wherever roads meet
Or down the sizable hill
up which the common trucks pull junk
with their irregular wooden bodies

            the dark visitor
                           straining
         to one side

                                                     c. 1952

    S t a t e

A drab America, with or without
advertising, is possible
only in this limited century

stand up and take it, don't lie down

Then downtown gloomy
as corner lots beside banks are
on cold evenings
              Many
things darken
jazz our classic narrow the network
the foiled bridge the drama
the static press gray monument
heavy between blind piers
polared and holed-up

the deck so ended

              (river-drowning
not daily be pronounced as history

ALTER yr
with the light Blindness lifted
Day remind me of all
 26 years
you were nothing,you
your parts had not come together
          yet
through the bodies of others
  they were dying and dead
 and they did not even have to think about it

and to all intents not possible
incapable
and much matter passed and I
have grown while talking
                         (surprise balloons

and I can no longer see anything much
without lying
although before there were many positions
     much gone

    to remember, thinking
(one foot after another foot
 one oak after two houses, one
  wind after five yards and
 those that circle the world

the stars
down to us
before and beyond, in the middle,
us, who have seen, to have us
with us
     and it is their privilege
        we are unable to get there

              Mars, after years of it
              Venus Saturnia

And I saw them going
                    in the hard light
Which was also a little weak, disappearing
straying, below still silently
ohm, seen from the bulb
above the stoop, gaping
round, and weak, and the force
     outside of dark places
dying out by steps

and those men, streaming
ghosts and the arbor freshened

springs capsules

precise water

or the side tops shone
the light kitchened the smiling present
abundantly like the tidy inviting trains

but into the plot a resting place

I then mistook the moon
for a different headlight

 near the corner cutting my actual sight

At the time, this park was a livingroom, the people, trees,
and without leaving any roads between them
myself on the outskirts

and the fir tree went over the house

July 51   # 4 1

         U n d e r   S a m e   W i n d o w s

It's a flash   old cloud of dust!
He wound his pitch up with a s-steer
and whether it hit or hit the ground
That was the time of their lives

Not polared by the sun
spin they laugh
and the dust laughing when they hit

and the hot grass
all the time fading it
          rainbow

  once even a sprinkler

and the stars were blinded

they were closed in

laughing and laughing

 closed

          L e n g t h

They went and
lit for the country
around:
                    Sunday
a big sign
edgewise   in the back
over good roads
and fields of weeds
hotdog stands
gathered cider

               the coast
where drivers en famille
were not blatant
                    and
farmers
        look
               northward from haying

EAT AT CHILD'S
      in the distance
by any means, changing
out over the ocean
where there is no bridge for us

HERE IT COMES TO US
or GENUINE PARTS
            I don't remember

past
the establishment
they never spot

and the houses
which
great and vivid
the eye at the corner

present themselves,
and downtown,

a daily course

A , Is it Serious

A book with a jacket
below the title having
   a typewriter, black, is
about what?

          Guess.

among good and bad it says
somethings
against the plausibilities
            (with anecdotes
of happenstance
Luck is out of the question

   no good for this sort of thing

  as such   a wild affair
                    might lead us anywhere

But that is just like that
doll of a machine
which after it had crammed the fingers
I had the idea of sitting on.

And as I say
It's time that deus   am I telling you
unsettled a few of these things
which are just unlucky

   as well as lucky

and by this very fact
the course, though logical is
    all wrong

and they haven't been treated right
      though he is very natty and
                    reasonable

so this, in spite of his honesty
it's trash
  and not worth the dollars or cents

        (and has a chalky pencil round
        and thick blue besides it

There are many things we do not know
Say possibilities are enough and more
we don't have to know it, which is good.

Jaggied potential, when it will come
Over what house grown headlong and palpable
Descending with ultimate speed, wind in the eyes

till we turn to our shelters confused moving away

and no-one can tell if any clouds bring rain

■ ■ ■ ■ ■

What happened?

            I've got to blow my nose

Mucous in summer

                after so warm
                        (Aug. 1

Spring so flowery in my holes

    the trouble is I have to get clear, you see
    as anything might happen and
        time marches on

De Limits

and how to make pictures of the weather
Nobody can tell We stumble
beyond the impossible cyclone and woods
 into familiar streets by the coast

or diminutive lakesides,through their trees
at the bottom of the hill, different from the sky
and staple shades like winged land

and while the orchestras still are present in my mind
the forecaster does well speaking of fronts
            I live in continual air

Which might round my self burst
      volumes of noise and
thick slopes blurring the smoky chimneys

                like
            ancient and foreign horses

and even when conditions are ideal and there are
still scheduled
                as many as thirty games
in the middle of the year you dread the fall
waiting for what follows, when animals must retreat
and the winter must be got through

  then, Then, you occasionally see
                the snow sharpen

        through certain windows and

memories looked forward to

                B

Is it serious, or funny?
Merely?

            Miasma of art
                              The

more the merrier is my view

seeing the levels of the world

and how easily emptied space

                                is

Here they made the perfect pots
on the beastly floors
the spoons and knives randomly dealt

and tread on the pine-cones
bare-footed
to cut wood

and here,the women went undone
till noon, plaiting

 Once this happened
and the cooks brought food to their seniors in wigs
in dressed-stone mansions;

I am omnipresent to some extent,
but how should I direct my attention

sufficiently to what I desire, to
stop, to
what is charging on the roadbed, what
          going away, the
fire-gong, people and busses

    and even in my room, as
I know
            the waving sun
                              the

constant ephemerals

b l a n k - b l

b l a n k

R e q u i e s c a t

remember the sabbath
                the sabbath
the candles opposite the ice-box
 are twin

            the booming air the
            tv

light blazes away
downtown in the kitchen arm

C l e a r i n g s

As history lays in the mind
   sudden houses of this landscape
I have watched going line by line
 blocking the rest of it
which over years I have seen
 but again it's as if time were no object
    raised while the eye travels

and who can say how a tree grew with
the sky in back of it, the
visible ocean doesn't exist
       really outlined in the night only
    the leaves crossing the sight lost
as faint elves in the known world

Or I am behind trees, wasn't I
always like this where
except for some nakedness of winter

or fall, the regular changes come off
as I had remembered
the trees still standing paused, turned black

and my road's houses, absolute hills are banked

all present greenery, turning aside
    wind displaces my sight

                    P o s i t i o n   o f   E a s e

Now I will do it, I said,
springing from that dream
 and how much has it happened

in space, grasping, out in the air
by those trees, the shadow, each with its spot, really
shaking down,in the brightness
                                was I there
What grownup has fastened them, then, like mountains?

Travel,
climb of the summer leaves
in the beats of rain that refresh them
under which they still float

                        bending,
unseasonable winds
vivifying them

              in their spasmodic journeys of wind

no passage
          access
                      inaccessible

Admitted clocks need not be heard

Who disappears   into those growths

              II

still is, a crash, that was
in the deep back yard alley
lawns, netfenced, hedged,
stooped, and a short parallel street
                          intervening
 only heard

        held, past, otherwise, so,
 in the arena a
beast from a soundtrack
      might have been advertisement
at that hour

          by the gas-pumps

O sound) there life

echoing

                    the neat concourse
you can only mark out
                    by not moving
an inch, not moving

                              the mind

Unhurt I imagined, the car continued
                                        10:4-10:4 1/4
                    treads railing the sudden cast
      whereas once I would like to have seen it

            denying it
                              such as rollercoasters' ragged ends
                              always glanced, or with less holes
                              flashed, struck in the news

now I have been honest I am retired

         tilt back
                    still at a point of safety

                    III

silent
though History doesn't repeat
                    the night, I think, coming
just now
            each of these years
       lights from that faraway window
and will, again,
                              nearly enough
                    by this door

and everywhere, on the other hand, I pose
       at one march
                    and raising with fractional eyes cover
another one
            darting
                    the same,partially

      If the grass does not vary
            or if building is thrown together
         how is it

               areas, smothering bloom

in the dark parted like branches

                    IV

Those atmospheres are far away.
and surprise mountains widen close
as the sun turns and flights are lost

Towards the positions of the poles
Like the body of land I would like to die.

This inclination of the cold
and lamp, the slope becoming fainter

Night facing outward end to end
those quieter stars, mild or severe,
show unroomed passes where they stay

   and touch the dark through background doors

Past hearts and flowers neighborhood
Autumn histories
                    story rains.

                                  no
       they do NOT come straight, no, they shake
off, much as the beams
which they may be said to have stripped, which still gale,
still figured, the air

  waver
A long time I strained, watching
what I took for walls, nevertheless
Do not let this speed fool you

       It may be perfection is exclusive,
its own season,
                    naked,
                         an Alice moon
        though killing time is killing ourselves
The radio warns the motorist
        speech from the middle of a room
but blind from a stationary point
                    twenty-five minutes to go but
                              New Years
he hurtles towards his Square

     Prepare for transitory hands
some stars have moved, later
      In the shifting fogs, the stage bound hulls

         fast, colonnade

                    M o r e

leaves, company in death
cascade to all the branches
  one at the top, single
              I thought I heard

                    what's invisible I feel

Wizening is essential to it
 Aged in the wood
Leaves being a rush, hiding
the faded principles, rarefy outward
                shades growing
  sightlessly to oblivion

  How many places the trees
  leave, somewhere attaining
  final weakness
                as if unmoving

  far from diffuse they
  flood the levels of the world
  limit   the ground, head-on

      the sky through empty words, bush-heaps

  It is a quietness like snow
  Light numbness of the mouth
            filling the window

  but there are no tiny sharps
  However, do not be deceived
  the world isn't empty

            (I am more idle than this morass

        street where maples cross

    cars in the middle lane

      dusk from darkness presently

        A comic leaf now stood
        up-ended on that hedge
        a slight inclusive mar

I T h o u g h t B i r d

Shifted my arm, my hand in my shoulder
stayed, but my elbow flat
and my other something else, a boom
on my ear, so I wasn't
any flier

                My head
though
unsevered wasn't
circle
            made
myself relief
against the bed

all flat agility

                            A
crazy flowered Crete
comic
Egyptian and
a big-jawed devil
Greek
around the
 Parthenon

        slight
        bosses slipping
        the march   that morning

The midnight birds remind me of day
though they are
                            out in the night
beyond the curtain I can't see

Somehow bedrooms don't carry
tradition I
and the boxed radio
is off. But what am I reading

inward performance

Has relevance. Allows me to hear
while something speaks. As for the bed
straightened by visible hands
only is it huge
when I feel down in darkness

Because the face fades from your mind
Mostly your own face, that is why it is new
these times you face it, in that sense new
and you hold on in a sense
ever leave go

on the walk, you here fixed
fallen on your nose, know
any production of a tree

however strong it is Once in the movie
Light was an art, faces became stamps
 but even they faded luckily

so that they contracted into vagueness
 after all including the clock's face
moving the wall, only the clock with its facet,
in the mind's dark made light of, back of the eyes

the back of the mind unweighted but pulsing
like its latest discovery, built by hands,
put to no future use

    & C o m p a n y
    G r e e t i n g s
As they've got to make
a living, Luxury
and the minutest
Advertising is necessary

Words won't express
How good it is and
really gets
a clef in every kitchen:

At Christmas, Thanksgiving,
The Fourth of July,
Betwixt well-wishers
Multiply

The Split-Pea Freezers,
The Dogmeat Packers
The Slimmest Squeezers
And Traditional Crackers,

The Pickers, Grocers,
Growers, Fishers
to stuff a restaurant
up to yr kisser.

Noise Grimaced

Noise grimaced
we took pleasure in the heavens
    the close sky
although we knew we could not have seen it
and the flash fell expanding the light
up the beds and walls at once
dying, leaving the star distant
although we had known all season's heat
        like a room's still air here

slowly I have sometimes heard my ears click
as if some naked siftings bared themselves
and who know how these needles come to the body

Another moment· Day passing or

beside it,
            out of the corners of the eyes
    the wind like the rain, it can't be swallowed
rain as rain, walls shut in
virtue of walls, Rain is a forest
but the wind is too light for a sea
    Under it still the skin is unquenched

And there are not two dangers either
none moving away, in front forwards
  to my head

though sometime it will rain, hail or
                        still more variety
gripping the shoulders
                before or after our deaths

Apples in the October wind
have become blossoms
                    and pears towards the windows
give a certain comfort

The background is
radiant light, tree-heads
shift recessions: boughs
toss through approximate regions
upward, violent gaiety
deep bays and bays with fruit,

not rained-on but drowned
by the going-away sun,
piled in the wind,
  season's onset

Apples But pears point
towards Euclid and air
for quieter elements

They thought they would eat, but it was a trap
Inside was a room, with table, sink, and stove
  but the windows were somewhere else
 and the little boy grew piggish
                    suddenly
but the woman who made it once forgot herself
and the heroine exploded her
Then children mostly danced outdoors
though sheltered from the sun and the moon

Road - side

The wind with trees makes lightning
and from clouds it makes thunder,

though not those

Instruments penetrate, not through the bushes.

   In some hidden street

while the world is flying, the maps
topography changes,   inch

relax sound relax   sound

                    under those contours

Sometimes the raised figures
                              deepen
and clash, wandering
to become pools or old nations

And this is the calm world
from a distance
Indian-open smoke

And these are greeks
both northern and southern imaginations

which are quiet and magnificent things

And never see stone
or North heralds

this isn't history

But, for some minutes, wing
moving at length

  crag
the boulder eye-pieces
in the islanded edge
trailing the tip

such silent drivers will never exist

              D y i n g

And yet they hunt the great whales
      the beauties they see
finally dwarfing them

Around the world
                  What's more
they name them, and these are not tags
but inexpressibles

their function

and even the unwanted,

and time

to think lower than
                  spheres

from the sustaining air

fresh air

There is the clarity of shore
And shadow, mostly, brilliance

summer
        the billows of August

When, wandering, I look from my page

I say nothing

   when asked

I am, finally, an incompetent, after all

formulism   autumn   the
 sun, cleared to
          hedge   The colors washed then

now striding silent

                  bridge
                   we going down, by
   these memories of

  coats and vibrant hounds

Here fall   Are they circuits
turns, streets

landscapes, open   New
earth or old world   Spring
began the shorelines grew

  dim   Heightening, Heightening

such lives   many comprising

   this is a proud way too

                                                    June 52

          T h e r e

You know,   the globe is round
so I regard the horizon

An unreal thing is not much
and so I'm satisfied

But
   What's that square
I always pass?
or down this hill even

         and the post office
cornered over with black cloth

been like that for five past weekends

  occupied with others
                    not the self

In the room the instruments go on
and are nearly alone

but sometimes saying the same thing
in different spots

relief, the burden of repetition

 make it a new time

or when some unite, there
            is a doubled instrument

            C l e a r s

Light retreats now from inside
And outdoors its fit of sense
 is apt to drive us, wild

no matter how we lift the blinds
invites us, lures on-
to days

  Too much from the earth
from the bare   earth
                        to bear

after suffering

                too much

summer Spring promised
                    overabundant
winter
            we steeled

        shiny
welcome   into our bodies

Last autumn but a memory
                should've swum, dipped

    once, in that blue offshore

   roll, grass,   corner you

the pressure from inside sweeps

                 T h e D a y B r e a t h e

to be worn,
                lightly
     be   in
                  continue
                  unhedged
   with no weights,but walls
                    no pains, or
     standing division

Here   an October sea;
                       And planes come
          hulls and spread they low
              the milktruck going business
putting   from the ocean they left
          black, all-black
          all-white, black
             up, low, under,a flat
                            bulge
             world broad
                   in each part, flattened

in   (charge

Under lea, deep side

The country isn't lost, unlost
the country   without fog
               though pstcards are
                    for the brightness

      Cards from here wouldn't do any good

    since unbalanced
         take twenty years

  the road   intersected   drives
  an island
     based like a backyard blind

but after twenty years

no horizon break illusion

           (other these   ends
            applied physic
            eye, remember
                     but
            I have to imagine

October run   turn
   with hingeless difference, The
     scarce made buoys

```
something
          tagged love
spread, though, always
coming back, will
      not be ruled, into

·o voice of Paris, Salom-an
                          bounding   Europa
  through the washing
by the turtles kept in the corner
      a few acres, her
windows, just at the walk
door, just at the stoop
          a short way,to the hill
  ending the row
  shortly to the top, out front


              couple at chess in the cave


  reveal


                  and she went out
finding reports of him
          again in the flower-beds
```

c. 1951-52   # 6 8


```
          I m m o v a b l y

Blazes the untimed room the rug
Blurred brightly, while another
              is colored on the air
 and one or the other is silent chewing gum
under the floor-lamp, reads; darkness
is indefinable and light sits traveled
dashing
                  and we're shut in
as if there was a storm, away from this
old hearth, hearth, it was draughty,
cold, as if it was an old cottage
in an old century, killing colonial time

but hear the music, gaily, from New York
```

            O u t   a n d

    shut down my closet, seeing
outside   partly
      storied,   and part clouded
          why should it be around me
then a sky going
                made in one corner

 beyond sight
              they don't surround but make a
                              protection
    shelter forward

          I am through glass
        till it should become   thick

        it is
                partly in back of me, it was
in fact   and
why should I have more eyes

        I can here imagine other houses

          emotions in space
once I'm crazy, secondly then
  all things

          a time for plowing

     a great light

     all things
                      all things
everything

and each form
                  so is it formless

  hug the wall
 easy
       have to search

          don't get it
                right   in   the   <u>hallway</u>
    explain all about it later

                      and neither must I rub

I'm not curve or
wholly squared
              (it is all around

              here

A C h i l d T h o u g h t , M a n , A
   C l o t h e s p i n A n i m a l

By-pass: the deserts
the emptiness oxen broke into
trying to swallow it
                    Inhaling salts
the man-trap mountains in which they dragged
theirs, over peaks

                    restless, impaled
Those men, fitter than you, flying
through inescapable rain must have remembered
pure dust in the eyes

        Peaceful Pueblo were Communist

Men and infants come a long distance

    the Romany Sioux thought them a joke
reliant and knowing nothing
                        Plenty
had grandchildren

        Belly-aches, two precarious legs
strung high,   but we have passed around the world

The Sparkplug, dead, the train, being stopped by snow
press on a different way. Danger
quite catches us, practically too much
reality shocks see stillness
here again
            the plane
lost in the dark, suddenly we drop
into a bedroom we didn't think of

instantaneously
                a man is failing
but believe you are safe

  (that is the only thing

P r o f i l

                    Which
is life for
        make rounds with the home women
                holding their pockets
                                from the ready immersant storm

it is
        an easy chair
                        it's
                    made room for
        as possible   somewhat they are
            engraved,   more than trees

  or all these seas like space, the shores
  hold past, steady as ships, half-standing
  taking distance as if bounding

Is it protective? being lost like stones

Though time is not the essence
                            they perceive

 and 10-year-olds sleep with their hands wedged to their hips

    and how many at once
    by accident

```
and the squirrel
                jerked behind the tree
   Once I could catch only the movements
then the face, bigger than it was
   area gone
             and yet the tail
                              both sides
and the animal in the background
batting his head,          crazy
     which means:  he was eating


              thing ugly and beautiful
          holding his lavish bolt
           like the bridge       most of him
          complete pride
               and the glide hobble
                 his green prison


stopped   led on
   his unbelievable want


       crossing the road


                        straight


     and he does not know


   he does not know


lightning


        the ground quickly as trees


   and eventually running in circles
```

                    P l a c e

below the sheep may be
growing into their dream

Above they may be mating
                              (like
this an escalating shaft this
 the light-retired ceiling

        or taking socks off
                              time's out
           setting something
already there   for the mind

then occupied

There was a story once my father lay
on the apartment's roof
when after marriage they used to rent
before getting to
their own flats   on the edge
                          If he
turned in his sleep he
would pass all these

And there was a slight tremor that night too
 something in these
 parts   rare

V o i c e , F r e e

 come to stand through
 intimate dark
                 a
 sympathetic surface

slide threshold of words
 by sincere, easy
   breath registered
                    a

   sober
   synonymous story

                THIN,   REALLY

everybody's color
 garing

                    the room was pink, the window
            cordial in the pitch

            love's
                            (power
            worship view

Grazias dark
And   now, to Brahms
And Italian
                    plush
                            and good-
                            night   the naked
in murderous streets

    among peasants   peasantry

                    (in foxholes)
when they crossed

The sons would be better

            and the new dawn   (precarious

                hourly

    the road does fill up
        with angelic infants, strolling

from which the strings run
         the globe in
                  pavements to ship's board

     what is going on
and my imagination fails

in the room where I was

              up the Elevator
          that fitted
  the plain floor over the Christmas loops
                     and smoke
in which I lived but didn't come home to
    while it was still in my lungs

          who, unable
               have never touched the stuff

and I remember, earlier at the station
where we were   sometimes each day
        on that road made with the rest of them
but had never stopped till now
                 and then moving on
               decided not to buy

which I think is on no line with any other

   and my head
portion of the air, moving and still

      T h e   C r i p p l e s

 The cripples are beyond religions
 although full of euphemisms
          we all live better,nowadays
trying the average lives
they manage it quite easily,   As well
know, in the ground
          what the feet are,
                    and still
what lying down is
                    quickly

and they may not do anything about it
    believing anything can be done
yet, to look at them, I doubt if they can stop themselves
                          from thinking
(and this old lady tries
(to help
                    me out

          rained
the wind blowing bulkheads before the windows
when I heard the surf where I hadn't been

for three years'pouring
     the dark was nothing
And shut my eyes in piles in images

and streams from the bay's fury
                    bottling me
walled, and even willows over the roads

  and yet a cat's cry was like a gull's
   crooning and I couldn't sleep

sleepily turning   Then
I found a thing had given birth

Last night I had the dream
 that comes once in about five years

It was a very romantic one;
and I wonder how it starts

we were making
          excursions of our own

    and I don't know where we were headed
    running to basements as matter
    -of-factly as curbs
    where cheap books might be good

    but we didn't quite stop
    in the unlikely places

        and something else, a
        further shaped retreat

    and there was a song
    after that they were singing
     I failed to remember

If I live that long
it'll come back
in one form or another

Dress for the Mozart Serenade
 I heard coughing out of the orchestra
and work for the organization

  to put this over, produce steadily
 at the front they're not perlite
  but this is
              both discrete and required

      and did he shake in front of the prince
      No, that was a
      figure   of speech
          the figure of the leader

          and rain   had fallen
almost silently rain
beat, rain
spatters rain
built a wall from silence

      around the trenches and cameras
          as I have sometimes imagined
      rooms   seen from some rafter
       pulling   the eyes   down

```
              D I M   V A L L E Y

               a long time
and where the future is
a near thing, or distant
               over a hill
you must turn underground
branches like leaves
 whirling inwards
               dark
     which can go


                         the storms are over
the perfect room
subtle as it was
light          and
  God's shadows
ranging their own wood


                  there is no bottom but hole
bunkers and


                    just indoors
the covered plain
and other rivers

eyes at cornices


                     flat
the animals ,   come
fixed, driving

all slope differently
     between the guns and
         hoped bombs
narrow hiding
       they rocked at the sky
up stairs
where spring was
               past the stove and
                           beds
       through the bends of a tree   grown
                              independently
the usual city
```

        T h e   C a t   G a w k e d
  high on the window

And the old lady died,the snow
drive in the air swaying the wind
blow
  so I couldn't see her blue house
        and passing people don't
quite see her, landmark character
walking, in the free months
            nor the children level with the road
        looking as though she didn't speak
yet as before as if she saw
cover up to hydrants the air
the hedge-lot invisibly layered from
her side,   quick field
held there in multiplying   up
      between fences, round our homes

    the walls
            or floors   rumble
nightplows, coming into my sleep
  the ceaseless dogs paused in a line
they don't learn when they play school
        the children
  in front of the sun
or the milk-trucks

bound
            brakes thrown
      home over thirty years, circling
back in the still snow
    the driver in his hour world

  now that the snow is solid, that can be moved
      for how much time
          and liquid, too, moving   first
nothing   room allowed
  the thickness   nothing of room
        it might well be the whole night
    though I've never been awake all night

how long, say, have I come to the plow?

E a s y

  yes, there were no heroes
                      where none were needed

     and people become afraid
     doing the simplest things

 or no, in familiar surroundings
 for miles at once
 it is put down to memory
 Shucks, it was only necessary
     I didn't know what I was doing
and they put it down to modesty

       The Age of Anne Frank

 Tempted by choice
 but how make-shift could they be
    when they were thrown together

yet had to die   quietly
 after all that
      left in the opened air

 it seems,   but I must only
  think   the world was shrinking
 steadily   to the diary
        though it let up
           for two days
 she had been away from it but she might have been taking it
 when it really happened,   that one time
 as at first they thought it might

   and for one year she lived elsewhere

         E n   S p h e r e

every lightbulb of the coast
shows up the citified world
at anchor like a concave ship
terrace

          whose bulk is the last berth with
endless corners when
welded against the sky

These moorings monuments
Behind the orange-crossed bridge
and after that crowd
          amusement park

The dark stable beach after
cottage cluster where streets
end open the dark floor

musty inside in back
the sheds
          hidden by light

slums, farther plains
beside the office docks
distance stacks and tanks

and one arm people in cars
or foot under
houses face the water

while stores at the Q-tail move
by starred and softened danger

                                        July 53

a slumped woman
 is presumably the height of fashion?

 At any rate, this is a poster

  I'm glad to see
  there are all kinds of posters

  for the moment

                                        105

　　Learning

to live while merely existing

Compound them

together more　How could that be?

I am dragged around

or my mind would wander, a stem

not very often　but still

a center of perception

everything

　　view

Dogs, old dogs, can't

move to a smaller apartment

to let the growing families

in. Are they

　afraid of the walls?

　　Hence: loss of efficiency

July 24 53

　　A　P r i m e

Until the wave of his hand
　his letters looked like gloves

striding　　　(Parallel
(the hedge　　the street

I know, eventually, he'll
come around
　　　　　　to
　　　　　　deliver something

            P r o p e r t i e s

What we saw was a half-clapped roof
the leaves' angle, then the height,
houses that didn't meet
and the hillside skies
for the 1st time

a wood, shale beyond trees
flowing over gables,
and the almost-deadly cats
to make the crossings seem plain

as parks recalled
for ordinary sabbaths
which might change with news
somewhere further than
the boards' fencing, low
or high,   surrounding a patched acre,
the drives shallowed by thought

Walking to the edge
or other ends of those streets
by the light plant, where
it smells,
            you see it the same difference,
the sky keeps fading
in a whole familiar setting stars
apparently hold still

The dogs troop, scarcely
watching each other
although with experience
   going along as quiet

feed,or attracted queerly
to their tails and behind
  or tangling flanks, edging
 round interminably, they come in

all sizes, and some look wise
   but you know why that is.

nobody knows what they think or why
exactly they break and tour here
as if it was a big trip
they happen to come together
at some evident corner, or a distance
near it
         they lift a leg screwily
always at an odd moment
as a matter of course,   despite all the tonguing they do
      to stay dry

admirable efficiency!
   and today they've taken it into their heads to run low and raise
hell with the postman

Be With Me

(slowly dying)

Beauty is immortal
  But it doesn't have to be
Now what about my chortle,
  which is more complicated.

      I'm getting stuck.
      All I know is
      Look at that muck,
              rising, rising,
      I'd better jump.

   Look at all the dark
    On over the wall,
   It's wonderful you're not blind
   when it's barely there at all

Turn to the Hall
Rather than the night sky,
It looks bigger
            Appreciably

You should hit the mark
 With so much light
        In or out, even
          Up one flight

I mean or need to be stark,
   So do you, really,
 Beauty must be familiar
  And it should be eely.

All things are more or less beautiful
   If we'd be somewhat at ease.
There are ants in my plants
 And oils in the seas

Strange knees:
                    I bend one and step down
My hip rides over it. Another, leg,
is in full view and ends the flight.
I stand self, ready
for my next stage

(in a world I've been through before

ANOMALOUS

His shadow conducted the war, after
Christian's death: Once grimness was granted
to his mind there was no danger

eventually he was overtaken
in the streets. Peace being
something we should be more about

But I like the shadow against the wall
in the movie. As it must be,
such shocking violence objectified

--from which victory stems. He stood
Long after the fatal wound in the garden
and walked to the center, fighting
sureness, among, others, on the neat path

FOR THE LONG SEASON

I heard the crickets seething like machines
October   may
the winter never come

        the birds

now in my age that the sky is timeless
 let there be no time

and the blue go down among the branches
under the bark green

If that is possible

or let it pass
out of me

        morning.

c. 1952-68   # 1 0 6 a

FOR THE LONG SEASON   2

five pigeons on the rim of the barrels
 they are tin and so rattle

 and it takes two seconds to get
  on the other side of the street

                    and there is the air

            sound does not travel
            for it can't be seen

            I hear them from far away
            the birds outline the world

    the pigeons walk in the air
                    as we swim

                while the leaves are blown

O creatures

                critters, we
            are the world in the sky

                the cats make themselves narrow
                 going through

OUT

day blots us, blot
these days named perfect

            harbors and these sails
and shores with their foods   that
adding depth

no complete sight
of where's the unmatched
long horizon
even with new maps
how you leave the coast

            by expanses and waverings

or the crowds, smears
as against slides

      and about wondering
      (and stars could be corners
legs, up
towards splintering beams

            they are making room with walls
(over whom jumbles the sky

The
edge of the building knows centuries
replaced, the gravel home
between these flats

            doors, slope roofing

      a cut through the middle of the hedge

facing town

or there's this tree standing there
and here's the wind

1952

O p e n

They nod at me and I at stems
Yes, I agree But I flower myself.
or can't change

Yes, passes.   As I,pass on the air
As i,   pause
As i dream, sight
 I have been on all sides
        my face and my back

Disappears any time a world can
Reality   dissolve

        abstract, abstract, O little
                    seeing that word
blue against the stack-
            o i walk i walk

the pavements
assume they are yellow

        the flowers seem to nod

D a y   S q u a r e

The dogs, my forebears,
my companions
 with smart ears

the birds flop
lighter than planes

and the girl has been serious
                              eating and sleeping
     the old woman laughs

N e w s   M u s i c

Dress for the Mozart Serenade
 I heard coughing out of the orchestra
and work for the organization
     to put this over, produce, steadily

 at the front they aren't polite
 but this is both
          discrete and required

    Then did he shake in front of the prince?
    No, that was a figure
    of speech   figure of the leader

                and rain, had fallen
almost silently rain
beat, spatters and rain
which built a wall from silence

       around trenches and cameras
               as I have these times imagined
                    from rafters
        pulling the eyes   down

114

        moving a finger, motionless

no Pain, pain

problems, thinking,the thoughts, see it's
actually hard to sit still
            they made up the attention

whatever I was getting

    The English professor talked
    they in the class room
    breaking in French

                (past the major chair

then there's a clock to be heard
            seemingly with no limit

  it doesn't matter if
  it has to be wound up
at the same time going around

     T h e   W a y

        applied an old woman the
sound of 92

        i will not say lady

  no, an old woman might
            now be white and tall

but wan, little and dark

darkish   --getting on

but could still scream with pain

        N i g h t   o f   E x e c u t i o n

Now there's no more of it.
suddenly, you've seen how it's all come about
  to the last wire
 and the "intent" of Congress

                    peacefully like
any accident, yielding
on the way, a worker,fixer of power
or connecting lines in mid-field,   peacefully
like the end
 at any one
likely death

or as noted the week before
Men, who barely escaped

    but somehow not again the movies
but the headlines, still

one might have thought it cd be prolonged

THINK, READER, IF I DIDN'T WEEP

    He saw his own face twisted lunged
    in too much of a hurry   Who
          saw moments of calmness
     rough like a rock one came
    at times he grew in another place

    And one choked like a bird, then looked
    (he had strong hair) Was he
    superior   and opposite
        the healthy people

    and he couldn't long be neither

          hell ,

          he moved on

E n v i r o n s

Many shapes of wings
on the sky and the table;
and large men carefully at dusk
lengthened by lights watering their lawns

turn, paterfamilias

   and the sweet hay as I go
   from one foot to the other
 more so than I might
 mingled with barber's tonic
 from the morning's shops
   of papers and bright rag
         as if we could
         take time out for life

  and the afternoon's seas, like yards

At some smell of smoke
I found a spray behind me
and the two on my right gone
  tending the grass, all night
 everyone beautifully
  (by themselves   the same thing

time   for the surroundings

     against the strip of hill
    ending low, a space
    on this side, hut for clouds

c. 1952-53

The Bible Is Greek

The Bible is Greek, I want to say
to people with romantic ideas
of morality Oaths are not true
The future is vague

                    But would they believe it?
Your two cents, they might say, taking another
pill

It would have to be their own revelation

Beauty's not taken rightly With the best
will no words make the whole universe
And what's best?
                    We subscribe
without knowledge

1953   # b 5

WALLS OF THE AIR

  Yes, the crackers still make
  an impression, even after
  the endless war

  which, if it ended, would have no end
  because it can't,   or be hidden

  Each burst lasts two seconds,   yes
  it's calculated
   although I couldn't say

          I can't see how it carries so far
  I was there before

  The grand finale overlaps, which is
  considerable
  producing an echo

  then a retreat,

  sometimes laughable a sport

What's to be done with it,
          until the heart gives away

     Why, children, children,
                              and

          the days then past
    grew,
·   and what
    was forgotten had not been known

the gauche, stiff boy
        why didn't he
know, Know, he
couldn't get married

     he lived near   her

  though, even then, young
                      stalking around like that

and such things   (few

 It all fades back in time
as time rose

     And, somewhat with delight
I recognized myself

(so already a sort of man?

(but, when the reflection isn't there?..

          W i n d

Put together
        but always carved
  the violin

lower parts

an oboe
over the hill

in strengthening tone

      and protracted stomp
then
          not wood

THE WAY THEY DIED

          the accidents

              almost the diseases

and men their old bellies
retired and so fragile
      the family turned away
  or, on the spot
    to enter another place
prepare us

contiguous, whether

      (the times and ideas
                  --and the moments
              change

      (and others you never heard about

A n o t h e r   O n e

the head, perhaps, bloodied and printed
each week,   and all my birthdays
the man with hammer and saw
 Thank god, pulling him close to the world

                              Fires and
from one house, confined to others
  clean, handful
or mouthful now at any rate feel
 more exposed ,

          exposition
Of snows Brighter and dark After they
were beaten, recognized, put on the reservation
they kept on being born,   so,   here
all marked with English, being aimed at
                              thus,

but under old treaties, never
emerging when we have exactly the eyes for it

So lovers, for what they're worth, still
in spite of the news of suppression, which surely
                         sounds
true,
      (nothing you can't help

                        the future
               through windows
               of peaceful moments
the times must change
                   by
               historical doings

and it only remains to be guessed
  what happens now or
    what you tie, or see

      how long

     make the room habitable

THE CARICATURE

man,as if out
 of a painting

in a blazer pushing a chair
in which is another, lolling
cripple

            (and the Epileptic is wild for a moment
              (like a machine   thin
            especially in the arms

                    and some times afterward

   scarcely, yet one of the office

   I take it for what she is
 or is quite likely to be

     yet with that happened face, her
biggest keeping thing

and the legs

                I sometimes imagine myself
movements, men

HOW THE BLIND DID IT

first one by a sitting position
                withering legs
finally in an instant

who rose, then, (his arms
after the(disappearance
                        c-o-m-e on

able enough   --in full view   but
            mincing
the first time he listened and
they guided him

he felt it himself, and columned

Is it dawn or a weird sea
 the music gives, or
reminds one of,   leading
      (only
       the sound
and how long is it kept

Now it is staccato and
now the notes are long enough
 (from refollowing instruments

   more humorous than wind

Now they are long and in
   a tangled, big room
  hiding
          and somewhere doors

now, apparently   (out
     original control

  (but with fingers and beat

  the players move

        H e w i n g s

After tall and blowing summer
 Or Spring
the deep, vanquished,

Around, not
    the descent
though
         the early or later year

            transitional

      something like Vivaldi
   hordes below
     the baring trees

  but not the other seasons   123

            C o m b a t

Other people I saw them
years,   and the roads
  all slightly different ways

so many places   near
the impermeable
 bathed this afternoon

now I think them
                hard to connect

  and the women who change back
  in some instances
                (the present opening blondes
    fast,   children again
      repeatedly to school

  (and growing,   like such times
  following the woods

 then streets
                a single car
  bodying such a distance

now I think them like the others

  Now elegant and ordinary
 having reduced all things

  the elegant is both

                (other places
        we've been to

  and will regulate this
                            fall

```
The sky,
   and trees like
  wind

           the trees full of wind
steep and continuing
posts    mute in themselves
           and conches turned lamp horns
might belong to the houses

    shouldering runners which
    all ways go straight

And the last colorless leaves
tearing as in
a gauche direction
     the same as those first, perhaps,
where the Spring is

   The lyre
    as the forests  making

   themselves
          direction

            joints
   between quarters

      only squirrels (not even the cats
             or some men, do
      have business up such grades

      stillness  it may be
        of one kind      and
             another
```

D a n g e r   I n   T h a t ,   T o o

Time and again, different, the same

the houses,   snow or/ and the trees

      fire   signs put at the distance
      (bricks and slick chimney

             time

one place to another, and

the present always is here

well a different concern

      *

      didn't want to be tired
      wanted to stay in bed

      could've been satisfied

      *

birds on a snowbank
    their shadow
    on a back wall
    shrinks in the dawn

      a tree reaches

    the sun a balloon

      the roof grows warm

A l o n g   L i n e s   O f

the movement, the 2nd concerto
through the horns loping the
 piano

   in strength the
drums with history
the stalled car outside

the building, shaded
nameless trees

building

   God

but the silence grows
into a noise

        for we
        live and
        it is not dead

C. 1953

I have never landed in the bathtub
but thought of it
            and dying

       T h e   W e t   S n o w
                           falling
                 brings on the horizon

         from there
the stripped hill
straight with

the darkness of trees
         thick
 and pointed,   and

the windows like
the backs of cars   all

modeled
        back

   with no one seated

under the porch

the pigeon's wings and tail look
       like a duck

   it has a ring about its neck
       the color of its feet

where it stoops
     always a place

                 and sometimes it goes faster

   the white pigeon
        (crazy and devious

 its eye, its eyes
     picking gravel

With the world a chameleon, I come
from the house where it kept me
Now the water is all aground
and there's a nest dropped on a crotch

beautiful storm. like a great curving wreck,
the light waves chiaroscuro how long
the plunged cars before it closes up.
upstreet the buds are springing in green

this is the sea
                and seagulls cry

                                        1953   # d 8

GRT WAS IT IN THIS AGE TO BE ALIVE

let us
        put our shoulders to the wheels   and keep abreast

 with Daniel Prork   and the
 exciting defeats our boys in   the

  public opinion of the great will tell
      through daily while

 we must eat
              her motto is
                              it
      every self-respecting sports-fan might
                 all the nice friends there as well
     be good

  you have our invitation

 to sit and relax, just
      take it easy and all
 for fifteen minutes over
     Hanoi

            ((of all places   129

THE HOLLOW ROAR

    by the sea is
          the autumn piecings
winter, the high-school
stood on its feet, bleach

in season

    it is an increase in the traffic

from some sort of silence
yet I think of the sky
something invisible
      flying in or against nothing

  yelling for the sake of yelling

  in back of the waterfront

     but a drop of rain is quiet

 the spread-out shore
    the shell
  picked up sound
   become mythical

        and dimmed too

  actually it has the wave's curb

      or from far away ((the teeth))

hard baby
     the present
  men   the children
   paying no atention to the game
)
          the wind is a tug
        the slip of a sign

                B i r t h d a y

Every-body was supposed to be enthusiastic it
 was a big hall with lots of corners
   though 4-square simply, stating the case
   simply, and letting it go at that
   and the girl who looked disgusting, almost in bed
   or was she disgusted, was
   polite, as might be under such
                        circumstances
    she said, you're not in the way

I had thought I was, with
her permanent small expression,
                            and
eyes, the wheelchairs had to
keep on the go, and we were all 30 or 45, time
always went by, Till all the
                eyes were turned
the true surprise, a man as a
hectic native .. doing
a strip-tease

        down to a "censored" in black

   letters, and many
were doubled, as well, by age

        and bits of mistletoe were strung up
        by the idea man with no fingers
        who had only time for that

        as it turned out
                        being volatile
        which was about as far as we got

The wedding, like the
lord of the manor

        giving them a send-off

   while she hangs up the clothes

        nowdays the president
        makes a speech every week

     sleep through woods
and thus even the hills)
                              buildings
signs, and what's under
(I didn't have to see

down Connecticut

suddenly biggest city
 in time,   spreading
like the palisades , could be gone
By pouring out south   west,   short
nearly
the whole of the continent

track
across the border, cross the vertical road, the bridge

That isn't central,
not in Panama or Pal-
estine has nothing to do with it
                              Second largest
but none is piled so, one on another,and
each from the ground

to see you must go through
strange   how street can close

                    the skies

since gradually the world changes

```
    THE RADIO

Twelve years listening to The Warrens

Their concern is:  Sanity


        AIR

                    and

one night I reached I
couldn't get Mexico
straight from Canada
```

HE MUST HAVE GOT UP EARLY

```
    The dog's imaginations
    are greater,than mine
     my fingers are nothing

     I cannot see the pads
     his snout is again
    a thumb ,    index
    for the legs

        not
    wholly close   and the tail
      coming in different planes
     or none, rather      with
    the hairs at his sides

    he is not doing anything
```

A CREELEY FOR MAY

Sd one (a socialist)

     POTENT BLOOD OF MODEST MAY

                        (pay
              said one tells me
that - and Ralph Waldo Emerson, responsible!)

down with revolutionists, down
with 19th Cent-
ury, and May
day

                  nor up with leaping & cumm-
                  ing
                       (sssssssss

          Some-
      thing else, some
      complexities (simp-
      licities no longer are
      if they ever were, now
      are source
      of ubiquitous
      errors

                Point is, how
                be you
                4?

                   where
                ahead - what
                may(cakes)?

A l a s ,   A l a s ,   W h o ' s   I n j u r e d ,
                              look
                                I'm no Cyrano
    this is slightly more

                    the 16th century

   time must go on
   but here I am

   and I'll come, he said
   should I live that long

1954   # f

it takes time to walk
around the corner of the house
and throw away the stone

     if it didn't
time would be a problem

I accept time,/involved
as I accept the clouds
and the houses

and the water regarding which
I am bedazzled
making reality dream-like
  and bright field
            continent

I realize I've
 got to make moves
even if I don't

135

as I held the mirror
the boy committed suicide

and the other man slipped
what I have done often

he's now composed

  himself, still here,though
 the world changes

        and it's funny, of course, that,
 all of us have blood

the dark swimmers
 their heads in the sun

     If time shd stand still
you can't see it move

which way does the river go
 partially the

 wind,   and light,   Down waves
      the indefinite flooring

the toppled clouds
the squared mountain

PIÈCE

Open the windows wide (half)
and go to bed

in the summer
with a breeze across your crippled behind

   whether there is a moon or not

and the sea, some
  (cover, for a time distance

and light
                from a remainder of town

wherever it be
before the coast

the sun breaks out from it
 The straight cracks of the ceiling
the shadow up on the fixture
and the glazed corners
   in to the edge of dark

end the thoughtless or
       crowded and figured days
followed by sleep

 everywhere there is dirt
 stones nearly

   under these rooms
boards creaking
with no free of cellars

   and birth, I was going to say
               almost too much
  were it only the morning,

      death
     ahead of us in particular
       though some our lives have encompassed
the willow wept in his eyes
 ham, lips as he
   strummed

with the sun on it
for its own sake, and the
cutting clouds
which do not travel there

  Going about under them

    --which you life sideways
       as if in thought, to walk, and
      not like an animal

my eyes went where there was a tree
which had nothing but the sky

       through it

             that place

  (beside its own leaves)
birds I might not have seen

          and I can't remember
          when it was isolated

In the midst of pain I think of you
  and the grips are similar, though

          which one will return?

     there are many
  musics, but you are a sight

  Other times I would like to be away
  from you, who are an empty idea
which first caused me to look, and see

          the straight face and shoulders
          are very plain

```
I look at you,and still there is time
respecting the self,    breathing and quiet

                the leonine man in the movie

  and what's ahead has its
  own) impossibles

            A play means to be cut off, however
sincere, everything
  else going on
 so it is present nevertheless
   will be for some time thought of

  and commonly parts of the world
  are more than the absolute whole
```

```
not like an animal but as yourself
                an animal

 and there is the figure of your age
                each year

   yet the body is still
  in movement, a direction  with no
  fluttering

      a distance

                appropriated

 so the human body is
 bandied about, places

     and going in the truck to the movie
     I felt myself a lump

                removed from what I have done

     the wind by my head
     like sand, almost my own

      and the rest of me, there

                (the road turning
```

Between my two trees
in the public air
            through them
        and the

pole
its still, borne wires
the planes came

at a finite angle
        without contact

        their sight

and so the day continued
but the sun went down

        and that night came
                on

I have felt it as they've said
   there is nothing to say

there is everything to speak of
  but the words are words

when you speak that is a sound
What have you done, when you have spoken

   of nothing
   or something I will remember

After trying my animal noise
i break out with a man's cry

The fountain of youth is a poetry
and whether we are one minute older
the present always arrives

come as we make it
According to our healths
(when we are sitting still)

but time itself kills

the brush, consumed or not
                    and the individual
which is needed) dies

                necessities dying out

but nothing ends
as everything begins

Life, for her, has become
  a politeness,very much
 held up

eternity
    going on, and on

        now where it started

  and mine is a similar one
   the variable

                    our barren loves
                    flashes of rank life

There are so many memories
 maybe numberless as the stars

                like the smells of washing

                which come back
                        and the angle of porches

    memory takes time
    and that is the trouble

    nowhere is it
    simultaneous

        and so i die
                    and so you live

THE HEBREW BURIAL-GROUND NEAR ALCOTT'S

 the well fit men
 still clinging to the old

 older than Brook Farm

        yet nearly strange

 in spite of the polyglot
 the cemetery is green

        marble with red bricks

   set the moulded curb

   the weighted light road

        the dead become eternal

every day afterwards I sat at the table with her
and said the same thing

                no, I don't need any help
                I can get the food by myself
                or I'll wait, I
                was never hungry, for food

I never dreamed   that moment

on my birthday she bakes a cake
        I wish I could do one for her

On the Wide Shore

        the seagulls screech

reared to the hidden
with interior

walls, raising the streets with fields

    on another side, multiplied

 the sea is forward
        the town back

   between the two points
elsewhere the sand mixes with rock

        the roads grow
        and pass unseen
        together as

hedge
the sea
 do not move

at one moment

     the sea having little wings
     under man's convexities
     from removed skies

143

Living, I would like to be
like Socrates

                    but that
         is, only, the vanity
         or so I think

   I have kept alive

   the sun rises
   and goes down

               T h e   W a v e

There comes an end to 'entertainment'
but the self, the dilation, is
always coming back

I'm under those clouds for years, now,
and at moments I see them

in day, around supper when it's summer
or the afternoon

for what they are and for what they might be

it took some time to know
they are bigger than ocean liners,
also the shores they resemble,
or the sky, which seems
nothing   without them

and then there's a small plane
that's always been outmoded

on the way past them   tipping

that's how it operates

Why that light should always be shining
by the door --even when the sun's out
 of the new dormitory
which has windows instead of inscriptions

or vines gripping the rough
and yet inexorable   in their routes
then is this a plane or are they stars
advancing, from my view, at nightfall

with prismatic dusk, weakening
   (yesterday there was a sound
         behind me
    bringing the canopies closer
      and so brief
      suggesting they were unreachable, or

      partially seen

or familiar clearing
if we could always be there
   the quiet courses of current
   through the blank labyrinths

the curb of a district

once more the scene held

the natural environment
of the cat
reverts,
in and out of the houses

the cars change
as the cat moves to and fro
      articulate

or cats   each step of a
world, birds
flank both sides a pole
curved on the hill
the wires became wing

        the garden bushes or
       random clumps or trees
        a way from the year woods

              the landscape surrounds the houses
              or the houses around land

                 the clouds fast

                    alleys between
          sometimes
        the doubly cut sky

          the open walls of
          the landscape

S P R I N G   N I G H T

spring 12 o'clock
by a chain

it is not dark

the moon
and lack of some cloud

or it is
                but the air is pervasive

        weeds hem and advance

        of whatever kind

            the crickets drop

    undriven from
    the field, line
    of the roads, the back
    yards
    not having come

    the cats
    with their conscionless tongues

THE WEATHER

Of all the crazy things"she said the
crocusses are opening

while the fruit rots in the
ice-box

    there's a fly in here
She was cooking,
        gas   the
sponge ought to be appropriate for
    the griddle

    MRS,   .

even the statue
is cute

    they ought to give her some lipstick

That may bring us back to Egypt, yes, and
love is free?

    logic,at least

        The Strange Land

Resting earth I feel
the different wind blowing
the branches I could see
  with the barest leaves
the stars and woods move
    and some weight comes down

                the separate trunks
        cast tunnels lying plain
            below the heads

whose shapes stretch and
            spring by the air.
towards the corners rail
shadows, the old houses

the busses of perfection
in the night deriving people
continue and some mount up
at stops from muddy entanglements

off buildings with empty windows
where the sun will arm itself
tomorrow momentarily

the useful drawers agape

  while tonight there might be an owl
  round some newly done back yard

            T o y   a n d

               the birds,crying at one another

        the dog has a head
         like I have
which turns toward the female
               as it happens they are both black

                         at night the green trees
      but the active dog is lean
      the shines of light
                    ridged

        she squats
        the way in which she was spaded
        by the door to be let in

        Near the beginning

she fed him peanuts in the zoo
which quieted

surrounded by a civilization
the bear and the odd monkey

        pawed
     at nothing
               the fleas in the meshed air
            their suitable hides

        and the visible flies

      the monkey businesslike
      the peacock unsurprised

           and earth
       the dirt was simple

the keeper at meals
retreated to dark huts

        holding his hand near a cage

        he supported the sun
        it had rained some days before

        and the sunset was cloudy

                As if Hearts Pause

There should be no turning away from it
 a neutral worker in the daytime
in my jaunty brim, shade,

                        rhythm for such a land
                        or the wet places

concentrate shadow   shade
keep flitting watch   over
stalk gravel and sun's yard
from way back
between the houses I remember

                        exciting things.

        and the fire burns itself out

The lion's viewpoint, and the fish has a
singular vision, his is the flattest
                world
sentient, that knowing object
light way at angles to that cigar,
 body moving and drinking

        the leaves' approximate hands, sheltered by fingers
bent up wrists the hard way
        and trunks toss fixed arms, some of them awkward

Or birds, like chafing dishes
or cry with fishbones in the mouth
    black, clutching an undersized wire
    near where the insulation dangles
    or whistling sharp spaces of wind
                work through the day
                    pulleys are out of date
    ridiculous
                and how the birds sing

            (America hums below   sent

```
            The Sweep of Dark
              far off

    the cat stopped
cold

                 pieces in back of the mind

and dogs ?
  even at summer

the high voices of gulls
when they disappear the sky closed

or profile of an eyelid
the asleep cheek, nose

                (there is nothing infinite because

                                wind blowing a paper
                to a horizontal tree
      outdoors
                                     like a shelf

            suddenly, and away   in
              some other moment

                      thinking it almost a wire
                      then not at that side

over the scene, before
the street up the hill and its houses

like a man's wings

    unknown, the minute still

  and a barrel tipped
            there with no sight of wind
            emptiness of thought

        itself

                and canted out
                          of the gutter
    the noise of barrels rolling
      unlike the sea
        the wind is all one way

      -sick

                  like the whole day
                  we realize is crazy

and the headlong cries

              (I always hear what
                the irregular times are

and for all that the cars pass

the god in the air
```

O u t   t h e   D o o r

way
        in the sky
and the earth
  the airy wind

burn) engine
without steam or even
whistle
   steady
is all over

        it might be visible

behind
            (a small quarter

inside, a soft drone

and casual,   afterwards

and it disappeared

  a dog's utter flight, chase of a car

  and a crazy saw

         at that time

   and hammers before

PARKER/ missing his last appointments

no tears
          dubious
not being what we came for

But against us and the records

  the rain beats
  a lower music
  down the window

and the birds may fly, before,
along the house

          (and his age was
           guesswork

          P a r e i l

But I have in my imagination tried
                         (that, now, at least, behind me
          half myself, lifted
over a thing made holy by future nights
                    the future always going

                                   elsewhere
                              untouched

while the lamppost steadies the finite wall
the gulls hawk above it
children and cats may cry

and again, out in reality
       the unknown car across the river
    and she coming in late
and the gulls wheeling
like any man,   for a time
             may not be

  sinister

But I, halted slightly
                         above
                              and as much above me
even while the wind blew up as it had done and
                the sun traveled
repeating thousands of nights
resolved many lives

Each   in Himself

she said,, I must really be getting old
I said to myself
yesterday,I   I
      seem to forget
  little things you know
every once in a while

      but she had gone to La Boheme
      I don't know how many times between what
      ages
      and she speaks of that too often

but many say this modern stuff is
crazy and just for
geniuses all you have
 to do is look at it

    and neither today nor tomorrow
    will she like dirty furniture

            and the son (incongruous)
            reads all the time

      It's October and yesterday
                          also
      she happened into an 80-year-old woman
       who was so cute, (spry), she asked
          all about the family

          keenly

    T o   S p e a k   o f

few human relations
  though the linen and towels
    on the reel, with the
              wobbling   wind under them
                  silent and unfelt
  while to step out,through the porch
                          and go on
  the indefinite morning
          lifted,in the present again.
      the absolute is a problem

and the joint of the room ,
shingles,   around which
   it is invisible

but room
        a morning and night

 and the kitchens next door
  in the sun

    the clarinet above us
like rock
        of some wind

    R o m a n s

the women with plumbed names are
imaginary here

          pure
      in their natural surroundings

      and the shoulders of men

   or the Greek dust
        in the street

          to contrast
      with pools

   while few things are very real

            plainly

      such as this is

and the clouds moving behind the roof-side
spreading the sun,
                              trees

  brush
        on
                    not vacant skirt by the distance

            wired through poles

  earth,   the streets
for the muddy land   the plumbed lawn

beginning a house clean
            a high plane
       around by the zenith there in
          the silt blueness,
                              precede the air
          a matter of time,

being gone
              and the low fence, steel,
     at this last intersection, lots
          for something
                          as if
                          stream-lined

      a barrel with strips

a tree passing the window,
     the closed room
                 another tree
tipped up to a window, and the tree at the back

aside between rooms
                     ash-color

hill
the formless break

accoutrement
   springed car

and some love

    look
                   the stars

                   and things in dark places
                   without heat

IT SOUNDED

 and tangled dry-   .

            like fire
        at the start of the day
            the engines
                    control
but the wind in the twigs
or thistles, stalk

        the birds are violent
        the spring

 they function by shouting

 suddenly

 all day

 the houses stand some paint in
 glass the dusty sun

 with the fresh air

 and the man who fixes the roof

 top and

 the transformer below

 nothing except the wires
 and the trees

        and the boys climbing
                    the shed
            (to leap
            and break

F i l e

while not setting me back have thrown me forward
the wide shield,   the screen

        along the Fels, the willows
               at that season

                      perfect i can remember

                         ` the tiles

    start a region of Africa

   park
        hills

     still by the clock
        the laid square

     the tree around in the movie

        the roofless eaves

  and come in after the store-front
    fluorescent
                      the red, spines in the play

                   when a child

               gas on the peninsula
               where the sea
                         not visible

          but at night

  (i still make a distinction, the tree in the snapshot
   may be the apple then in the morning
   sleep naked   when there is no light

   blocked by the kitchen boards

similar truck and so it is the same
                              dump

        turf and grass

   now is an eternity
   like ones I can remember

 from points the enormous reaches

     and the only thing that tells me different
     is
        words

           may you bring microscopes
           into the field

field, the only place

parked in
shape, so

the air parted, they are quiet enough

     now

 equipment appears
 and becomes standardized
 though not yet

        one with one light on its shack
      the other a long nose with stock, dummy
      on each side, strapped,
      a roller up front,
      the first with a blade underneath

 while I don't know what they're for

        the noise they were making

S u m m e r   w a s   G r e e n

   and the sky pushing outward

(the hill beside the wire
 the bough trees stood past
 sight of(the)poles

Crowded with   conveniences
  Out the gray back were the fronts
  of other roads

but the houses rose like living wood

     a horizon
 between the trunks

 the clouds coastwise

so what if mankind dies?

    the birds
 the croak and whistle
 has no future, either

so what?
so what?

the future arrives

the end of a stick
in my crotch

toward the speed of light

over dead man or a living woman
        or eating bone

and in the day-time might be seen
who walks the street

            they went clean-eyed through
                            the nights

        swam in the ocean
        the disappearing bay
        the green air for fish

        lanes of expensive God
        corners out of the sky

        and carried the dripping roads
        into the allies and piles
        such walls forming the ground

                    at a straight beat
                                clang entrance
            taking the idle air

        even figuring time
        which before goes by itself

A WEEKDAY

the foundation waits (will rise)
between morning and afternoon
for a 2nd load of dirt

the trucks move

eyelessness, uncovered
windows, the outdoors
                toothless,
      the garage
 open like a grave

or a child perhaps

           faces play, have played

the quaking stone

          they have wandered over from the next lot, their
          bikes   a near way

          slowed the gulls

 (a surprise, the difference of time

soon the walls will have been wholly
real
even on the hot nights

  though they were not always the same

```
          Peabody Sq.

               D r a g g e d

still
the tall bodies sinister
with their arms back
open chassis

      ballfans or
        floogie
      the well-made trucks

   harsh in variety

                    I saw the way the gull stirred
                                   with his brain
                 I being the one to sit out
                 in the car and read
                 a dog and old lady in a fur
                                   engine
                  panels going all over the place
                 the trees were like the Indians

                 with a round Greek room tangling behind them

                       (the horse for a weathercock
                   speed, atop the stables

                         still further out of the way

      the dogs echoing
                   straight mountain
                                spasms of sandpaper

         the cat folded on the room front
                        from downhill

            and in the middle of the square
            the road become a walled land

            the birds leaving before
            shock of the monument

               fast fainting the colors of the air

               desolation of gold

         gulls rear to the dead
         sky
            against the turned cloud
               under in the wind

               past the width of street

               my business being to taste the dust

               tree and the dry goods
               in the stoned glass

               and the men with faces
               down on the walk
```

To My Mother

so now we have a new bread-box

I face myself in the mirror

metal, the old box
was tall

and I saw nothing in it

The Movie of It

   Man misplaced   depth
   in the sea we cannot
   go back   through

   and that death, which is,
   ultimately modernized

                                          2 0 , 0 0 0
        now poisoned,the water

   a different weird light   l e a g u e s
   and music in the tower among
   the beautiful and oppressive

   fish and weed, shell
   blind sight, the heart, romantic
    solitude   odor
              visible

   violate, the
   weed suck
   of the spasmy creature
   vine in its multitude
     exasperation and reach

                and in the jungle the hirsute bears

   while from Europe the narrators
   escaped, as in childhood, destroyers, again, to
   face the blast

       grand

    (sin)

      pride

                U p

in the vague field of the sky
a track a moment visible

man opened
 his world himself

        himself and the world

the sea
  horizon lost
        farther away

     across it
the white trace
I realize the sun
 by moments my eyes
       bombarded, as yet
       my other selves

   And against any color
   the black speed hidden

  the other stars are pointed
                          in twilight

         WHO KNOWS JUST WHEN THIS WILL END

Space a meeting, so
when the wind blows
in the chimney
 the bed creaks

and keeps creaking, while
the wind flies
the clouds passing
over land, the roof

   nevertheless, impenetrable, as if
we put it there, it, still,
stirring perhaps, over our heads

  where we know,
the size of different rooms
projecting, discounting the clocks
      we needed, the shades hung

by the air, while the wind sails
  out in the dark walls

Night for a change

Outside the window the house
was bare, like ours maybe
nextdoor) then all up the road
within we were half naked, the
sides naked
    a different matter
 may they never wrinkle or bloom
 and crash

                the upper dimension light
a white rain from evening
clouds
    perhaps the second of invisibility's gathering
      to go nowhere
                        let pass

If it increases, tomorrow the ground
may be wet and stick
I will not forget the flowers
in the fields which
still lead one to
another   walls

        though June has been like autumn

a schoolboy sprawls in the
strange bed above
the fixture, and in the middle of the room
let alone the sun
the sky isn't to be
soon   childhood
simple enough, spreads on the corners

while the holly bushes wave
in the breeze or the tulips dance
      moments
            against the yard as the
            cat has been edging through

          G a t h e r i n g   N o o n

Only the outdoors

and from inside the building
  the lights

come on the streets

          tragedy for damage

      others you see
in the living rooms

out the night as the stars
closer apart

and what may be in their minds
is a different ordering

      as before,
the causes of their positions

so, somewhere, are the clocks they have brought
to be restful
      and the freely-progressing cats
  they accompany with their eyes

They inevitably go to the bad too

but the trees end off at the sky

and it would be a good thing
to pass, even
our own goal
till dawn shuts them out

          and we keep more behind this
  way, our yard

          S c e n e   E d g e

seeing the surroundings let
    the dead tree live

    again, you, liable to stare

    in spring as
elusive growths are its eyes
                over arms weighed

the icy reflection
permeates
winter
            the fixed wood

but springtime the tree opens
so the ponds lie still

while with the wind they move as they can

When the wind's flowed there is summer, a
lolling, maybe too much
breath,   the light spaced islands defined

except for the pitched gulls rounding
  out of sight for
                    another place

              as a tree
                a house
            levels

and the cold follows up

            A g e

The street was a hall
Lairs in the mountain chain
the weather shifted over
and replaced
    the lions or goats climb the ridge

windows admit sun
the earth is still plain
under the feet on the ground floor
clouds enter, moving
at a distance, the great doors
lead in and out to the sky
the little paths across the earth

A woman at the corner sells fruit

Do not put fish on the ceiling
but low in the walls
with the hunt
after you have eaten

        T h e   t i m e   f i n i t e s s i m a l

hills are monuments enough
and the grass, then trees and flowers

but the skyscraper is necessary
even before it is built

the clouds are radioactive

and the sky-god becomes
the earth

father and mother

ourselves   surrounded in blue
lit by the sun

I take the counter in my hands

    we will die
            in time, and in space live

            turning faces   soon   169

     M e m o r i a l   D a y ,

What's gonna happen

   a baby rises

 on every pitch

  slowly
     (coming out

oh murder she
  every second
 bathtub

      (and the world's running
              cars

      especially here

       the oil floods

    to frighten him
    and dispel the fright

    there is nothing to do
                but

leave supper in the raw

it's a double -header

        T h e   S h o w

Lombardo under their arms
the girls pass me
not paying attention

I write   the
impersonal and personal
keeping it up

        there is no special reason
        at all.

            the song ends
        from the upside down

        so I am caught in the pauses
        ten feet, over

        my head

        and yells

            I n

The air charged heavy with
things by themselves
and together,   the
spider conceived
as cubic machines
The strange childish beasts
threatened in self-removal
the jungle, and nearer the
                        ground
 the insects
consciously hideous
gaped
the cat climbed up an automobile
and there were no birds

    and I come back to
            the bare field

            of summer

NOW AUGUST

The rain is partly a hurricane
some south
    on approach
realize
how far
it is come

        south

the wind bulges

  and the storms fly

 to New Hampshire

    clouds

the weather's reported

                for once, again.

   the pennant called off

            the pavement

    in New York
                    where none might be

            no lightning

       a violent thunder

        two days ago

    by the sea, waste
       night getting wet and

           disspant

```
I said come in
but the rain fell
past the periodic chart
                        the thin level
                        holds us up in chemistry
down the roof and over
A mountain ledge
        The rain made it
partly that way

    the blue piano
    slight


in the distance next door
upstairs              oilskin


the boy returned


and i said let it
            come down
   the west blot
```

```
    THESE CHILDREN ARE GETTING RESTLESS

My foot hurts, the skin
elsewhere

People have a habit of their aches and pains
 themselves

                        people,around here
I and my brother are becoming twins


 and we step on the starter and bypass that
underpass

 there are pains it is no use
 I can't sleep it off

the flood
the beach ,   the chair ,   my flat
hurts, my
toes plain in the

humid wind, my
shoes are comfortable
```

    A S l e e p

air is mild, not quite
bareness, the sky
                    burning its way
the clouds are nothing

                          the rain
 is tremendous   it is mild
   dispersing figures

   the ocean   day
   break   the gulls
   manage the view

   a year ago here was a hurricane

   to stay in one place
   at evening

   to move about
   the morning pass

   the gnomes stop their shaking
   and convert into flowers

o laugh

   some, visible

   dissipating seeds

             to find more endings as a tree or circle

   one state contemplates others
   and we have gone in towards death
     leaving, up, the
   filled birds to the sea

THE BUFFOON ON THE ROOF

the carelessness and
immediacy

will

  the king
          in his
  uniform skin

        do anything
          touch nothing
                      or produce?

      there are all types
      of an animate gaiety

Before setting, the sun on my eyes
the grass at my feet, so silent
the wind blowing, the distance, waning
space
          it will be dark and silent
in a nomad country
                        dank, air
sound to the river
gullies

          i walk to see
        stars when the sky
takes off into nothing

the fields
      turn, waving
        forever

occluded, a slow jet
enters, fields are cool

at a distance
the steady lights
halt where the wolves wake up
and cry
and the bulls were shot

W h o l e s

For a while a year is a long time
as things increase in their number
    and walls break
familiarity comes

familiarity of life, which sinks
to a level of sorts, space

        (empty except for
        the rabbit's-hat of things

Before crumbling, the walls streak
with some tangent of minutes

and life takes on a size

T h e   S t u d i o

Who wants to be more
famed than Shakespeare a
little boy was

darting, from the gutter into
the alley, a seagull screamed

at the bakery, over
which a dancing shoe flew

out the window

in front of the neighboring fishmarket

            E T   A L .

Thetis is

          the opposite of

Pollyanna, the happy gods

But that is her way

                    of getting what she wants

Habit, but sincerely, while

her son is sorry

not for himself but also

a different man

like himself a twin,

though he knew this before.

            x

Their bible is a dictionary
nominalist

desert of words

for there is a time and a place

and the simile of religion
vanishes in the streets

  I pass the church 7 o'clock, she said
          the bus

                A g o n e

The world under the sky
clouds
all winter and summer

                    a snow
 descends and occupies the ground
to the stars,   air filled
 abstract wings

 on crystalline lines

                        and time between the stars

            a broken hinge, by the garage

       a flagpole mainstreet

       five cats have yokked

                        the world
            can't hold, really
            too many absolutes
                            but I am shattered
                    and another time lost

              while the sea
                    fans
                        the wind
             or lags

                      an old woman's shoe
                        flapping
                                on the beach

     and the awning was still there

b a c k t o i t

The good things go by so softly
Themselves it is our strengths
that run wild

The good and the strong,   dissipant,
    an ob- jective joy
                              sky
is empty   there are clouds
there must be sound
there

  the horizons are nothing

                         the rain sometimes is not
                         negligible

         out on the sky
              the other direction
 growing until it is nothing

there are mirages and numberless deserts

       inside the other house

lines, broken curbs

                    travel and distance
proportion themselves

 we must be animate, and walk

turn, abruptly

  the lines are irregular

Afterwards

I should worry if the roof falls in;
        until then give me some peace

 It used to be that the heater might blow up
 well, now I am the one who takes
  the precautions against that

            --the ones I used to take

                puzzling, like
                turning my back to it

          me walking by one end
          and the cat under the ladder

    (somehow I have gone through life
       without being kicked,
                         literally

      in the meantime, let's be asleep

    T h e   F o x

Old Volpone was a glutton,
   He certainly was,
He didn't have mutton,
   but he ate a lot of fuzz
He knew how to guzzle
And to muzzle and nuzzle
But life was a puzzle
   And he ended up with nuttin'.

        A l l   I n t e n t s

once a man is born he has to die
                        and that is time, the
        position of the moon

    the earth is never still in one spot
            or perhaps it is, it is
        (part way

                        it is round

    and we are always here
                        though every second perhaps not

    but here we are, we are

the stars pulling various ways
                        the birds went up
        to settle on trees

        many of which crash

              F o r   S l e e p

I depend on the stars
and the places of night

This is what it is

intent space, and
the speed which is light, growing
past any shape

the half-door or the door
slightly open

  this is what happens when I move
(or I see motion, all of it

      I'm in it

  the world depopulated
  those configurations of spirits

scattered and gone

so to disappear

the side of this road

                    nothing
    I want room

G e s t u r e s   u p o n   s c r e e n s

⧧ for my uncle joe who died ⧧

more than that:
here today at any rate

complete room, showing
the image
        solid or empty

            the act

close, the past is no different

                    might be so
            o the walls --

            walking man

        the figure
          of certain age

    comparatively, that is, to the body

      air goes thin

            times

```
 g e r i p p
            Wind

  · his ideas are playful and
on the porch   hanging
   as if now he couldn't move
in or off
                              charges as
far as possible          there's nothing else
                 Hands on the stick-gun
                                      and
      a harpoon,
             almost dropped to a stream
mount a solider ball bat,-quick
     he puts it aside
   it looks like,      slash the suspending rope
in an out-o-the-way corner of
        side,          over the rail
  so low           how practically
improbable, he's half
touching it from the hold
  his arms,    gingerly it seems

        time

            as may be

                 he's slow
  his experience is few
```

```
There are many causes of death, and I have died many times
I've told her that when I've gone away

 and I have been born many times
 in an instant

 but this death
         as also this birth
   grow
```

A n y h o w .

Life is a farce, so what is death

not even the funeral
or much later, stones
            and weed

        the dust in the road

                    and cold snows

I have become used to this
    my shoes hve been the same

I remembered the sky, or yesterday
            to look (most of the place

    in the afternoon it was old

                        light, made

        the next hour, dying, the
            fire blew and the engines
            roared in, putting on,   speeded

  Again,the
        sun gone down

    grown in the shoes, which are full

    the sky changes
                in ways I did not think of

    notice
        and others remembered

                    T u r n i n g

The world of white lies and little sympathies
            a level effect

      different Snow comes down
       or the sun reflects
          the jagged spread
       stone weeds, wire
        but ice crashes
                or it drips

   glass
                  footmarks

     sound
            from the invisible air

          metal flashes on
                          unexpected

        the cat crunches
        then licks a paw

                 the sighted main field

       glazed

                  the plant
                   broken in its earth
                     and dark smell

             a weak support, the dirt-grained
                 and gaunt leaves

                 pottery
       out of an element

M i l l i o n e n

millions,   one by one
MILLIONS, a long life

                 caterpillars'
centuplets   a
  life
      distant
 brothers

and I played chess out on the island
                    with a machine
woman

by whom I was licked
 19 times in twenty

C o u p l e   o f   Y e a r s

 Nowadays they call it a disaster
            snow hilling the glass
    a spectacle

landscape
topography, stuck
on the storm window pane, sifted

in masses like little hills
held out at a short distance
          or the long-falling
  shallow and cracked pieces of ice

like butting shaggy bears
or an animal fight
               on all sides

the billboards deserted
which makes the deadening wind cry

                (it is always a children's world

   --then a day after
   the snowball legs and battles
   the fast sun
   late slowing in spokes to fall

and there is gas for frying eggs
        under all this

                    S t e p - w i s e

The sea dances the heavy lights
below the wall; a distant
crash sinking,   matched changes of color

strain and confusion, out of which the storms are bred up
after this hour, hunting for sewage and spells
garages and the back yards
where the arrowheads might sift behind the woods

              hammering wings   the
              hutch   the
              boat lifting between houses

   there is the screening of loam,to
   leave the rocks out, pitiful ash
   crumb in the dropless afternoon
   of wine-cellars, accents
   of ancient yeasts   and that wire
   slant of sky filling our eyes
           blind, to run back
   the beaten snatches of dust through the rain
             or violent cold echo

They hunt clams In a lull
at the sewer outflow we dribble our own banks

                  dwarfing tin
            and blocked sand whistles, gouge
              quaking
                pebbles floated in the night like ghosts

bird-speckled, The wall reins
the barren grains of sand, bareness of shadow
the mud levels endlessly stilled

           awnings endowed serene

   Then later
             to return and
   pop balls on the empty brick
     and mortar, (the dirt stirs, the sparrows on the
         nest overhead in the drain split jaws
    as the sunset, in full, passes down

           P r e m o n i t i o n

There's a distinct possibility that no-one will be able to
reach any of the beach by the middle of summer. This
is because of the rain.   there is so much snow
        which pours like a sea. Nobody will be able to
get wet without being chilled. Most people will clogh, mud
will blow in their faces and there will be no swimming. They
will retire from vacation and sing
in their moments of strength
like birds in hot baths
        They will use up the community
water supply, catch the rain
      if it holds out. They will scrub gutters
   Will exhaust the common cold at the grocery store
         the newspaper a guard against typhus
      School will start in December

   There will be bullets everywhere after the frost

To learn something more of their environment
  in general, they will study hard
     and in between time look out glass

  Sometimes the rain is warm

but the walls are so naked
she said
I could hardly
  breathe

the bare universe
of leaves and
but the trees grow
stoppage

the air feels raw
the bird

under the
plaster

and the notched brick

the rain is nothing
but the walls

knobs

hangers
        frame it

the round beams

  cuffs

c. 1956

-22-   Piano, String

  It is
  A runny pool somewheres
  that is a beginning

  Dancer in sheets of
  unconfining rain
  eddy my leg.
    slightly pine spirals

  a cool erotic
  sitting metal frame
    and bells from nowhere
    straining the ears out

the ragged lines of
Popeye the

fishwoman's king of the world
while Titian's Europa lies
on a wall

the trees are wild sometimes
the clouds are safe

it is a leaky day

but what does safety mean?

    Élysée

He stopped on the irreproachable sidewalk
 the woman croaked

   Ah Paris, he is a good cook

 And after soupaire
 it lights
 yhar schtumach

 it's just as soon
 in the afternoon
  une lune

 the dark insides
 of --

nuage sur le champ

 the eyrie tower
 cyclops at the zenith
 du bord

    sink away

     the pitch on the meadow

  there are distant blackouts
  within a minute

 race de vivre

 the corners been far flung

        S T O A

there is doing and seeing, variety
and sometimes you even stop

and closet your eyes   there are birds here
and dark smells which don't lift

meaningless sound, but both unattached
and continuing in itself
whatever might your thoughts be

whatever it reminds you of

sunlight and darkness, trees
the wind roaring there are leaves in autumn
smoke blowing one way and another

and the folded snow is sharp
                        dirty when it melts
                             in green brown
                                    the black
                                    days

.   . . F I N E

how would you like to go back
to the stone age? students
 farm hands and collectives

          her story was told with dry eyes

 but they said: we wouldn't, though what could we do
what can we do

we couldn't go back

 immigration, from Africa, ha,
to Georgia? wherever

 "the beautiful isle

  the days grow old
      when you say goodbye

        O l d   M a n

two big pigeons on the new roof
below which he grew corn
                    ten years back, one year .

            P a s s a g e s

sunlight drawing from shadow, up and down the street
the dream of joy is only lightning
in the finale, beginnings so far from the end,
the short millions of poles, clouds on the sea,
the sea of human things the
leaves of men in the pure wind
of the seasons falling and swaying
        over the world land

and the pitch of the open night, the lightning seeming to rend
                and twist, the shadow to close in
above the flower the world cries out
time is obliterate and man turns
the false dream, missing details

                    that man who was deafened

we go to bed. The airs are dim
aside . marchings of men
and after this the boulevards

        the grounding of arms

    toys, and the blinding gulls

                a g a i n s t   (v e r t i c a l   g l a s s)

The indefinite world,men building bauble
  the earth outside   passing light
 reflected long shutters, vines
                        cars change
      pictures windows summer and winter

                          lost wind   yards
                   across roads,   back
      in the woods to the beach   water lying in the ground
                             confuses   a muddy paw
                          springs   random joints
           excitable fork, at the moment

   clams,   stick, to china, poles taller than families
  even cars make islands from isthmuses
     then bays   while
                  somewhere the broken horizons
        descend   the inner wall
          benches in sand or continents

   Egypt and the west away from the sea
                              with genial boundaries
       deadly, stinks, honks
        of the geese, gulling on wires   the
         barren preserves,
                          fish, through
          miles ending the world

              facing towards the land and the city
         reach in its own
            pockets like
                all fingers gloves   police
                  bank church jail
                laundry sand post office
                     brick   courthouse
                     somehow new in the countryside

               seminary behind hilled trees

                     scrap
                 heap of paper
                              smoking leaves   .

              package opens and shut

                 evening sinks and where
              people light inside
              the city spreading different directions
              to foot the sea
                a girl tricycles owlish eyes

I am a machine for walking

who can walk

the fly is
    complicated

she sits and hears the wind
                coming

  looking
        out

  The girl
  is no marble

Keep me still, for I do not want to dream

I live in this house, walls being plastered
all my life. the apple tree still standing
my life built, the minutes keeping on
the walls cross, standing around
                    a distinct company
    projection, the clothes wave
            briefly, touch beyond eyes

weed the garden
the light burns away the street
the peaceful corn salt in the empty night,
among chickens, sparrows and dogs,
the pigeons limping easily on the roof,
the cat sticking his limbs through the sewer
his claws agape, naked
pondering

  he goes to sleep and wakes up
   he plays dead, hanging ..
            rain melts
   and hail fans on the wind

    the thistles, when they get old

  nearly everything gets in
  and then we close up

        the flowers are hidden lately

            N a r r o w   S k y

Looking at people's faces like the clouds
against the abstract reproductions
and smokes , changing ephemera
 I am indescribable

A false world, but there are many acres
in a half hour , quiet
other than sirens

where is the city's center? As if it took
a map

            mid-air
I try to stretch over the ledge

having destinations, but no names

or over ten minutes, or, actually, 45
that is, now

        grass patching a cliff down
        beside the sea's wall

   earth crashes, crashes
        velvet rooms

   it is space enough for the famous

                we thought the boards would hide
                      . . completely

pretense of horror, till horror
comes, confused

but uncomplicated and demanding
there is no reason
 for it, you don't know when

Suffering or remorse is
better taken away
 for it makes a difference
no matter who keeps alive

 though as before, in pain, it is me
  still blinded, the sun
 now on the floor

        bones giving off memory

Some music nowhere; now
I can see this
man standing the bared stage
shearing his box, or is it himself
  his bow and arm.
        no space between I'm
        going this vocal wood

The continuity of beginning all over again
  then, high rote circling
like some seeking bird then   starts again

barnstorm, what shall it do Where should it go
raise a spire to the countryside?
or hit New York   Pungent bedrock
too plain beams. Lugubrious cut

So many ends its
    wonderful theme
developed no more than can be

                Where the bends

The rain opens up
          artillery
      breathing
        the whole wood
smell of the earth
      even paving

          softly
          reflections they create of
          distance source
          column one
          single of time

      in the air

          stone running
            field

          grass
              acres

                    (where no dimensions would seem to cut

    climbing the flat houses
      except for the roofs

      wash   the garage   car
            space
        disappearing
          the breeze way
          before the old windows

      so the appearance and heights,

      low
            windshield mirrors

        any ways
                so fast
          almost

            the park dim

                seven blocks north

                      nozzles
                          back

                  a view through trees

          (a n y t h i n g   e l s e   o r)

You can't be ol factory, you got to be a visionary
A goldfactory is what we need
to keep it up, to in, to out
we don't want nobody to run to seed

The trees are in their autumn beauty
but I can't stay still
You over-run a car the water
and it has to run the mill

Air,senses make up a fold perhaps
with the fivers and brainspan
though when the rain turns hail flow
Everybody runs who can

The snow is down to forty picks
the water's up in flood,
What are we doing with ice and tart
And running in the mud

T h e   C a t ' s   E a r s

  radar whiskers

          turned around
          following sound
          but stand still

so you think you'll GO there?

another thing coming

it's the street or nothing

I with what I've got now might really be good to have a different kind

          it just hangs around

        yawn in his limbs,

          Q u e u e

puddle long
in between shadow

    and that disorganized gestalt, dead?
    flat

            crossing streets

        I spent the day drinking
        just as if I was
        down the beach

    The sun ducking in and out
    as I understood it

            no fish grained skin
            water
            disappearance like mirrors
            a spherical world

        make the leaves fall
        darkness
                    in grassy fruit
                juice

                above through
                the trees
                or a traffic island

            motion elbows

            or sweeping ground

                    anyway

            T h e n   ---

To this paper I bring my arms
thinned by the paper, my own

            the dead of a Saturday Evening
            an acquaintance of my grandmother's
            the cigarette-ash and console ads

    reminding me, walls, of real flowers

        paper, tradition, a hundred years

 and wine in the cellar, for some
        lively occasion
        since there are no
      "happy events"
    and the old papers
    no longer of any use
 in the damp morning
    stare in the corner
            the thick piles

    since when?

                a height

                            hazard

    I haven't lived long enough

    who would try to remember
    how they tried to fix up
        in time the old fort
                between charges
                subdued by grass
                        making a close row

        the subdued grass

            the suave
            with no meaning now

    the green curves, far away
    from where the rat peeks

    there's nobody around
    me led outward by the eyes

1956   # r 4

          children's sizes are indeterminate

then there's those ones across the road
they live from a lawn split by a driveway

--well, let's go in, the kitchen someplace in the middle
the tv in the corner down the aisle ,
the basement window shows the circled grass

the kids have a dog that's ownership
Where he keeps his hat, they sometimes put on
they push the sidewalk for four lots
and
          take a diaper car for a milktruck

so a year is a long time
the snow more reflective than the glass
they see coming at moments in their minds
  and far away,the trees stay bare

in the fall the cats will spawn, usually
and birds come out in the sky, the nests dry
like crusts, and plants in the earth, fires at the gutter
the hens smelling the chickencoop
or garages hot, ragged water and oils
they rake up the beds with their toys

202

Couples

Those walking anonymities,
Nuns   against
the Renuan holy man

the night has some billions
if you had a thousand, eyes, the world would still be round

these are blinders

   the blind look up
   the blasted old jaws

        (ribs showing through

  Like the squatting boys, at the party

     they are naked at night or
             the blank sun
                or should be, they should be, though

to clothe yourself, you
                          when it is
    uncalled for,
                  the change

  the youngsters with shoes in their hands
         bare legs, the tightened pores out
                    coming back from the water
      which sounds after them, skipping a few more rocks
  and butterflies
            in the wind, the heated shade

          D a y s

Just like when she was little
the cricket sang, but the
sky was remote
this summer
        the hen-yards obsolescent
and the walls often not very wide
the bed a ship to sail again
yet more of a ring, dissolving in the waves

she tossed from side to side, there was
nothing under her, there was nothing
under her, to feel, she had gone too far away
 .bed,and a quiet night

The clouds went over, the trees grew
                                  out
covered, different from weeds softly off earth in the
non-violent sun

     broken)

                        wires stay on
                  carrying messages
            of no content, but   steady

the birds roost

               she had moved a moment
             the 13th floor
          the room all fixed
          up the stairs
          to the roof the
            grating
             old heat
                              outside
                               the walls

                smokes, matches simultaneous with
                idea
                                        change

            the cellar, all at one time the
            room

         phone by the window

      to do anything
      across the country

     voyages
        somewhere near the beginning

the rain noses in front of your face
when the clouds thicken, the vague increase

            gives you a silence

                  though widest are the blue points
            of the ultimate reach, taking itself

                  to the sides   wherever you go

            below which the hammer-thin clouds
            beach their imperceptible ways

she lies at the world

in thought, as before

    looking up again, without need of a bed

                or thinking, where there used to be hens

      fallen asleep

                                                    1956   # r 8

            s a m e   t h i n g

she will remain as she is, and I as I,
        that is, almost as she is, little by little

      as much as we change
        it's surprising, insect time

      time being an insect
      never mind that the ants run together

      the sun passes, we move but
      she is as she is

              C o l o r s

We bear our past into the present
as by our action there is
a simultaneity

    unbroken, for a while

 but the butterfly is like us
     shapes
         and
               quick
   catches

bearing ourselves out of the present
and the vague past we can't be

   if we ever had ourselves,
                 tight   open
       in the whole of our
                 knowledge

                 but our placid selves, waiting
                 to be told
                             until 21
                 is there anything to do

                 climactic
                             band

    the birds taking flight around us
    we walk around
    what we have set up

          the hotel sand
          is beneath water

       Y

I sit still, as philosophers do,I guess

it must be certain philosphers
have got used to the insects

      (a day in one position

    maybe the only way out

   or a group

     and every ten the
            same
     energies

the end
to the season

the fly is huge, it is
20-point primer

the flies turn how many
dimes on my body

are there, anyway

my body
will die

some other way
to kill

          M o t h e r s

Very careful the

children over their shoulders

                    (as if stifling
                              after all

               close up
                    afraid or blind

   facing the back

up and down steps

and in and out always

shirts

as if they were always pregnant

     I envy your clean knees

          T h e --

After two years I had the 2nd
dream
          It was
important
          (/if possible
 to shake hands

 to confirm it again

 or something

     I think it was the other one said it, hurriedly which

          we had done

the quiet of walls
  and between them

 the sky is rising
   or windows going down

      trees grow
    unlike us, in the sea

                    pail

I t ' s   a l l   r i g h t   t h o u g h

it is too hot sometimes
   and there's
enough cold too
      wind to stir up the branches

things are wild

But look,
the sunlight)

for three days

it is autumn
this time

          I n   a   d u l l   p l a c e

Mostly naked   a businesslike --
     calm and disconsolate
the violin, giraffe, wandering
                 the devious land
    less and less conscious

Finally the days and nights, they are able to
    come up

 but even so it is strong, though unsavage, slow

   with minute poison, they stab
     punily, stick after stick
     until it fails, already
     dead, the train eaten

     they are hungry

     time is of the essence,   2,000 lbs
       for the whole town

     nevertheless it is the priest makes the
         first out, the trial, such a
        battled creature
        to be brought low, so
         mysteriously

          by a rough calculation

              it is good
              meat

‡‡ after a movie of hunting in Bechuanaland
     by John Marshall of the Harvard African
        expedition   ‡‡

210

after all the singing faces, you
with your mouths out of sight

as i respond
Where are your purposes   you have kept
childhood in your hearts

each day,   and the sky was blue
          the sea was a waste

and you have come back again and again
   with the years you were able to
        come from a great distance

   Today my brothers were here;
   now at night there is you
        myself under the sheets

             But I grow old
             because I was too much a child

BRINK

       the less I
       take for granted

          the world going forward

                 I am getting
                  no younger

          an illusion of this
                   no, a

           death

announced
               Sometimes a squirrel

           affectionate dogs
           nosing in spring
           off the corners

                   cars, carts
           on final levels
           stretched up

                               and the overhead craft
                               in all weather
                               like windows

                     Whales
           conduct a feast
           near the cold used surface
           aways like floes
               the broken-off scraps
                     smells

               the huge climate

                        o a lively day
                   keen
                      light, imperceptible turn

             coffin of justice
                      among bottles and fruit

           the beach I hear not quite
           the next road
                                  dancing

               pavement of threads, things
               horns bicycles   papers
               on hands

because the street-light shines
steady
and the leaves fall
like a few stars
throughout the night

and the trees moving their bones
in the wind
which doesn't need light

the cold wind Lethe

the strong wind they sleep

the objects of a dream

growing

letting their
hands, such as they have, down

they are unconscious of
the sun

A response

the muffled trees

    Later it snows
    that is, after the
    leaves and the sun

        Considerable time
    variety of paths

    through the same space, thickens
    and piles up

    what was maybe fog
    when the sea smelt

    and came back

    as it comes back

    now

    the tides

                the sun spinning
                the moon having its
                different sides
                the world
                hardening

                    the trees pore
                    white under the shadows,
                    the fading, loose sea

          G r o u n d

today the rubbish truck
        has a green body

it is autumn here the leaves still on the trees

early,   though distant morning, forenoon sun,
                immediate struggle, bent
            card, cans, boxes,
dusts, a toy
shovel, a bottle, assorted pages,
wrapping, socks, the iron to a mattress
                but no bone
                or, since the war, cat-scraps

          there was once a hound burying one
          until he placed the right barrel

smoky straw stamped out in the wind
packing   parked minute

on minute
              as fas as I can remember
it has always been full, the eventual stations
progress
when it's about to rain

          the green slats again
today put up like a wall, filling
the gap in one side

            garbage long, low and slant-roofed

            and the ice-cream goat that reputedly ate tin
            perhaps in Bolivia
            a clean pediment behind

and they all used to dump out back of my house

                    the loads piled high
moved in the wind
          they stick
heaved up over the shoulder,
            like hay in a nest, stomped
down, ashes, that barked music,
                        however

apotheosis

      idle from
      the teeming field

          pin buttons
        the queer shine in the weather
        to rust

```
        The river of waste
     swiftly, the rain speeds
         and slows up

     not like when I was a boy, change-over,

             the earliness
             as tomorrow
             and the next day




                                                    1956    # s 7



             W a y s

    in the ad was somebody something like her

     so to turn away would be vacuum, wind

    Indoors, the sun not, this time, in the picture
                     flat on the page
       like a nice language

          the birds sitting in the trees
          weathervane an Indian shadow
                  20 years

         so many dials

         and so much rest!

         the gulls flopping in nothing
                               figure
                                  while they cry
                                          to continue

            the branches putting sleeves into the air

               moving

    ecstatic or something, over convenient toy

      the front edge of the picture,  my hands

                               straight off

                   broken    ( the backed-up moment

         rain on the fingers, trains of an age
                   a similarity                        215
```

so there will be no one
like her   so
we are the last of the race

          innumerable   and the weak

          David the King
          of the golden west

   I want you, she said, and I turned
   but that made it the middle
               of the desert

          with the trekked maze of flowers

     the cry

     a long tail

          M o o n w a r d

They are driving back and forth
I turning the pages

a real beach scene
with striped pants

          the radio it's
     only noon

     cuba and so forth

     til south
     you must take to the air

     a warm grave

T h i n k

Think of me. I expected to write
on America's failure,and go on living

        among the laundries and bread shops
        the busses over the holes in the country
        the mute-cracked levels rung with lids

the coloring sets   hot earth
box-car cows, white face, circus
mad latches

                truckloads of beverage the dawn
                burnt off the cut woods

    how much farther are they burying the dead

                        a compact likeness

                    the eyes hurt
by the lake smouldering tires. Breasts   the bark

Radios in the battle. think of me

        the slowness of death

T h e   B r e a t h   o f   o n c e   L i v e   T h i n g s

I n   t h e   f i e l d   w i t h   P o e

                    yes, Wolfe
this harvest, harbor of stars
the up-turned mirror in the window
earth   on my bureau

        the blank face

                        pale and tremendous
        dawn, blinding
        eyes over the sun

   sodden and unfamiliar
   the hours change
           to the south

  a man's proper stature
                        project

        I've been a bad boy

     no personal god,because
     we couldn't settle down

             too big to
           ride rails

                    freight

       it's true, at the heavy back, all of us, those
          tapestries are light

     your face forming
                    too great a height
        into a grave

           a hole in the lawn
           or the brick steps

     robins may eat worms
       or fallen leaves
                    the suns

            work

         to have a good
         time

      all
                together
    a baby comes fictitiously
       into the world
    he seizes as concrete
    Milestones the caterpillar's

```
inch
unable ever to gauge

                butterflies

    and the thrashings of man
    making the seasons heavy

                              the moon thin
                                   as may be

               bees

  they sleep

                  bows of the spring

  again

               fish
near a rough tank

      steep
            inland

        behind waves

    the piers splintering
    simple pieces of light

            That lump of a moon, in the sky
            past   like anything you want
            complete
                 all seen with different eyes

        fading off slowly, halves

        by halves

              divided windows
          bring in the shattering depths

    then clouds

    I think what passes over our heads
    are the huge things

                    lightning, blind

    split

      naked immensities of the whole

                  the stroke of it
              bars over the street
              and poles no higher than the leaves
                         branches

                  time intact of the body

                     invisible extent                        219
```

Leaving myself, I leave eternity
God, Melville said, nearly to begin
yet the moments are undivided; window-frames are objects
occupying nothing
but plain space

        streamlined? hardly, you'd say
except in parts
and a little odd, too, and
            always both sexes way
inside, millions of islands, as
rough an element as we've got,   but
            Wind, there are other things
like stripping and handling parts
as we find them, propping them there
to be more attractive why
that fish, driven all over
by it like a storm   by which she sailed
enough staging
to float on, but not with their wives

        a fine business, even so

            whatever size you please

That island, too, spread one white eye
which we give it
if we can

                (caveat

  the parts relating to each other
not even the absolute

The sky was empty, right above my head
    emptiest of all, above the gutter
when the gulls passed on
        with no particular smells
and the leaves held to the puddle
reflecting the wall thin window
                            the new house
   like a junction, complex craft, tenting
the train railing off
        where the sun blazed on the stainless door
        for a couple of hours
   below which I couldn't see
I couldn't walk far enough

    to stand over it

  those leaves about the first to come down

    Identify the earth with consciousness

            they were lost

            standing

            for some time, time

                    all those points to the compass

                    the weather arrived

          by such a manner
                         painting on over the sun

          the landscape brought home by sound
          noise

              the jet spines spread in the sky
                          there
          is the waste tractless?

            of outline no possible
          but somehow it's hard

                             circular   that's
                       event
              but the permanent gets more commonplace

            quick

          moments pulling what memory

c. 1956   # t 1

H e l l   W i t h   I t

another pill, another nutshell
The quintessence of time was the present
Now it's all bent in the sky
        sweeping the windows it admits

where the strain of arms have died out
in the living room the news flash
of death and the ways of celebration
beyond the growth of composite sense
in the lost orbit of waving dust
the sun fading and the big stars
hung from nothing a step in the streets

to the hum of a vacuum the remainder falls out
            graying
  the 12-thrust car muffled in glass
  the light shine deep in the road
    which was faced and always ran off

  and static would be fantastic now
  when at the bottom of the earth

        the atmosphere of woods and bushes

221

          T h e   S h o c k

men were connected with animals
I look up and see the plane
 scarcely

able to move while casting
my legs

I cry my world full of the head
if it would do any good

in the twisted path, not by distance but
                    the wind in my face

the eyes tossed back, fitted
 locked cars

        passing, coming singly to every one
              what is "aboard"

      beasts they wrecked, and the world still spread
      and in more and more ways, but back
      gradual,   as needed, faster
          and unfelt

              for protection

                  the dead brains

          and the fall, where, for a time

            the great matter at the end of my soul

          the dog deciding to bark up my feet
        and all the trees, with the wind
         dragging its roots
              blown to bits, eyes that are stopped

              the love of life and death

. Cantelli ..

In the shock of flames
the roaring cremation
 I saw the other people
  orchestra
  pit
 the fine wire
 broadcast the
 barely existent aisle
 with heads of luggage and
       tickets , die out
      with no thought
        or the easter hymn

    What happened the forward glance
      in this moment do what is there
            his strength just as you wanted
      beyond the 32nd quiver
        of said bar

          how life flashes
        and one time
          it has no place

                          look at the sun

      the instrument
      suddenly for the field
        grasshoppers

          for other investigation

      I suddenly might walk
        and might see
        the barrel opening horn
              one side

              even a clearing of ground

      yet no cows lying with milk
       in a little while

      or a smashed hood
      under the weeds

        P a s s i n g o f f

  the bus at the clock
              the schoolchildren
he walks away
down the street where
        they grew up

  in some hours

the wind blows

  at the other street they've
        painting for months
  Sundays ladders

      apply behind the open rails
              the sun reflects
      above on the windows
      the porch chairs

    the snow not less familiar now
    the year round

              time for the
              cold to creep in
              even if the sleds
              were not fewer

        the fire whistle
        at a turn of the head

              and the birds some
              in the mind
              the trees are just the
              same age

              yet free of that light
              morning and afternoon
              the hardened lines in
              repetitions

                underneath
                the shade and invisible
                momentary sounds
                even the bare branches

        flood, the beaten continuous
        source behind and further
        against the field or like a surf
         whether you're there or not
        the manifest and ghastly

        making a difference
        while they wait

        the houses that might as well move
        or might have, it's the same

he goes by
at a steady pace

the nights simple
but maybe as long

                                         c. 1957   # t 7

                 THE LONE STATE

                 It's saddening to see
                 the break-up of life
                 What is a big plane?
                 then there is sitting still

                 with all the unseen things
‡‡ movie   shadow in the sun
    Giant ‡‡
                 the old men
                 baffled and
                 shaken
                     on the way to their assumptions

                  the sky, earth
                  dust, or

                  the frivolous lace, or
                  history
                  the strong nursery light
                  above the long seat,   swimming
                  without a hole the

                   rippling oils   ˙
                       of the battle
                               pound

                    in the well crooked street

                    the glass

                    empty in the window

                    against the country

                         sunset
                       over with

                     the seasons merged

                     In the respiring earth
                            variously prone   225

      T h e P a r t y i n t h e F i e l d s

broken mirror of the landscape
even to the sky

men of the definite movement

a part of the river

it was an ideal climate, and

        it's too bad

            they can't die

        like the sun goes down

            young

            but, anyway, you have to leave it

                if you go on in living

                but, there are different
                kinds of natures

I like my friend's house
        with the driftwood picked up
        near there, right on the beach I'd think it was

                        two steps down
                            there

        almost resembling something
                on the wall

T H E   S T . B E R N A R D   L O O K I N G   A T   T H E   T O Y

he wishes he could
 but

well, he spends a long time around there

the man comes up
and straightens him out

                it's quite the ball..

STAY DOWN

Too much too little opening
some days you wake up and say this is hell, it's too thick
 Everything outside is empty

That's morning, an isolated time
you don't even get out of bed

while the big pipe goes in up the street
but the room's there
despite the invisible

   (twigs by the window in the next block

          I thought there were things in the radio
          like the tools in grandmother's attic

          thank god there wasn't furniture

Then the houses I used to bare my feet
the perch overhead around the corner

                the cigar in the toilet
          the gutter oaken from last night's rain

the birds around the corner somewhere
      the piano's dust in the other window

sometime they might have been under his hedge

            The window
             bathroom reflection sky

          the trout rocking the lake
          with no color but sound
          before it leaves in the stream dance

   roofs only with branches

             cars wait
      the long folds

             plane

     at night on the road
     downtown before glasses
     making it still narrow
       runless lines
                 build up
                       drives

     bushes at the pot old corners
     the ground to the sagged wood rough
     drifts fanning the endless stones

            the squares part up the hill
            gears

                    -looking
          for the quiet police

                         the basement station

                         archives
                         loan detectives

          the clothes don't move in the air
          heading the alleyways
            or above the neighbor garage
                              sand suits

            no wind in there
            facing the other room

                                             c. 1957   # u 5

Association

Thought
against death
          variety
   death   no-one can lead

   the stars death, a current
   dream, where it is night mostly

but there is no death, for they were never living

   the burn

   the points
   like death

          I t ' s   g e t t i n g   t h e r e

outside no brilliant colors but
 the winter's landscape
  the trees still bare
varieties of each other

          themselves neither open nor closed to

 the cities of the different world

  become smaller, under the snow which spread
  in all the routes
  by the thin eddying air,

  and which turned itself, a partly-visible thing
to drain off, yesterday
                    there is no sound left

when it started, the curves softening
 as the block moves around but the
  noise   the stone in the gutters
       flourishing tunnels

 the caves ages to implode, igloos
quickly passed around the hills and the woods
 with only a little wind, which is elsewhere
                    --no eyes

          and last year's trees
                    to be washed

behind which is that sky showing through

    above the beach

   the free-
          way

             shoes
                oil

    the weather   shingles, plate
    down for the highway
    slum plants, chips,
                    lanes
                       racing

                          exposed
            wind, length of the docks
                 the harbor's teeth

      square gas-pump on the corner
                disguised (rust-proof
                on the way in

                    the bare trolleys

The tree, swirling, the pitch
into the sky, the twist
from the pitted land, the houses
with easy chairs
steady equipment
the shades
wash
    the radio cloud
    masses
                    even in the garden
          of gigantic head
sometimes for the moon thick
beer

                    with the wire gone

      over the woods to the sand

the leaf shaking like a cat
              newspaper

      bundles over itself

      the night of dreams
      in which we care
                      walking about

      the wind invisible in the picture

              the yarns   cut off
          between the walls

                  stray beds
          and shelves, loose
              spades

          the ground rasped by a truck or
          bulk

It's H e a v e n w h e n y o u
          have billboards on your men-u .

   What's the difference
                      it's all over

                  but it's not, it's a
                  jet trail
                  which fades out
                  according to the wind
                  the tired tread
                  a segment by the road
                  where the sun faces
                  the cape cods and
                  ranges

                    with brick steps

                                              231

                or the time thunders

                    as clean as the new chimneys

                sprawling,

            bits

            everything spread out

            and an earthquake is accidental
                    for all you might care

                                                        c. 1957   # u 6

    P L E I N

            out in the wind
            space But a rainbow?

                        What is a bursting color?

        The edge in the room
        and it was wild from
        place to place

    close to the sun

            haywagons and
              different sounds
          to come
              to the same thing

          touch   to be lost

                out of the Auvergne
            country, for example

                            singing to keep the shack

        not dying   but the lonely
              sights raised

          you should have out an eye
          and remembered how that was

            we can lose so little

BOXES

The universe is a machine;
we are machines But the mind can convert it
the past built up by the mind
immediate

                    how long can it keep moving

                                        no longer

                            en masse

or is the window glass, or is
the air there?

     Memory or what? What is it? the
image before we were born

the absolute, scattered into the

                    cogs
               the crazy parts
            machine

 in the 18th century the gold sphere
was barbed   a future of bright
factories of the spectrum
            helmets of the intelligences

vast as it later turned out
in Poe, etc.
and Verne. complete
    his sub
        the human provinces

     in the spray of the stars
                    and sovereignties

          state of the mind
                         infancy
           in books

                    turn in itself

                    the governors

Glass

I forgot, and lost a part of myself,

I remember, and it passes away

                A nation, or lotus
                cream, ice, the
                tremendous gulf, or capacity,

                            waste

the field of vision
with the eyes shut

The life she missed, under her eyes
almost imposing itself upon her

              Everything needed   combined
              appeal   standard of life

                 the signs themselves   decisive
                                  directions
                 disinterested taking their part

                 net of the city

                 their torn status

                  like cloth planes

                 by the wind

Around my shoulder, your body
in full view, under the
light, blinding, of the dead sun

                  your mind, contingent somewhere
                  to the face, and the back of the neck

    When you grow up you don't see
    the small birds, which are still there
            where the radio now is

The nursery room
Outside the wild beast
lurks
          but that dichotomy
          is far off

Who said that sleepers shrink, they spread,
they spread out, though they disappear.

            Who would want them to disappear

they sleep hard, the brains
are switchboards, the colored wires
mean something

exactly, for them to enjoy

     The death, that throws this other woman
     into the arms of her neighbor

           --figuring things out

   it wasn't thought before

               grass and smoke
               grass and matchstick
               grass and gasoline
               the russian
                       rain

  she came up with a cut on her nose

                                  c. 1957   # u 8

    Pure.

on the 60 mile highway
The sign, Falling stones

from a five-yard cliff

Why shouldn't we get there

blinded to sure speed

   the rotary canyons
    inscribed   bare speed

   the countryside

 one blade of grass
     isn't enough

      and burned-over stars!

    the wind at the sea

 building, the railroads
       tension
  on a quiet Friday, smoke

  the blot hills
     interest to the blind

     like the random fires   banks

235

Place just right

when I came to the last milestone--imagine
stone--it said
 1620

America has died out
on its endless highways

experience piled up
fast
          here we have the life of Faure
for one man
               every
which way, the mirror
and the world, clockwise ...
for with that there's an opposite
for relief   for a spell

and the roads become wider
or lead us over the 2nd stories

                          a child's body, smooth
                     and squirming from its excess

                     mind, simple and not knowing

speeded, the mounted edge
all the slums grown factories

                     long woods of beer, cognac and rye

and there was the usual crowd
all sorts of builds, different

looking like all the world

and you couldn't imagine
                     the multiple space

    endless
   as others were out of sight

and there was an old-type ship

                     "medieval"as some had it

possibly with ratholes,   the
universe might be profound

                     every man's vessel (again) his home

                    Between us

I don't want to seem like a fiction
therefore I don't ask the boy
for the magazine I lent him
a second time It
                    never comes up

                he's always brushing up his car

to have one queer thing
is as much as the world can get

T h e   E l e m e n t s

  Out of the saddle
    his young head
blinks up to pedal
the rear wheel

But he thinks
nothing of it Steel
through weeds and edged grass, while he
  rides up and down   the front
jolt grinding to sand

spokes. it seems

  to be as simple as feet
 and he has to get ahead

   to look some more and come
  back   wave something like the sky
        sea
                sand
as though always wet and dry

   and swimming, his toes
        another day

RURALS

On all sides in a T
houses invite forwards

further on doubles it
finally   between

         the nearly floral curbs

so, knowing they have the double
these ends

and the rear asphalts the clotheslines the
grass meeting
the brick sides

lead really to a tangle
of few bushes or wire
hurdle

the poles, of an older street

instead of the grounding hills
or more across the open
                         and
from the way you came

         the straight passenger train

  except, one hill where the whole set
        is put out
  the stem, barrings, points
  the slate country road the only thing

 that avoids

   Grand Canyon far off
  and not to be rounded

     Way in; a tree-hut

   still here
   no fences, no   no fences

                                                    c. 1957-November 5 66   # w 4

                    the first to get it

  In the spring suddenly light the trees
are green and round prows, the birds
seem to like the gape wires
firm and continuous shriek
    tossing mattress, back to the sky

in the drain there are still nests, the light
from next to the grass disappears
among the crotches, leaves, and the sun

spreads someplace The
        hard shrubs would fold in

The man changes it, the saw
dangling to the heels, in the air
  earing the trees, pales the sky
where it comes through, where there's no other birds
--and where are they now-- for the trees must
stay green

    no sign of cancer yet

        RURALS,   2

savage the earth, the mother, squirt the grass
You're naked, a fierce burn, sun of a man

the temptation to touch
        because it
itches, or may be
about to
                after all the value
    done, the diamond
                splitting mad, King
      which would be life

life being old

you turn and raise flowers
as if on a wagon, strong
in the violent spray, against poisonous
weed and the higher creation

                attentive

fragrant dropping

                    wheel the barbecue
    as if the outdoors was a hospital
        as long as the stars should miss us

240

Off the house back
where the cat walked there
suddenly a road

   no size

              through, since
always going somewhere
              the bushes
          (but slowly   they don't
 interrupt

his body his body
not curving much the street

       suddenly from here
star

      or from that yard

          suddenly
   (how that was

no size

     (other thing besides space

  still there, not able to forget

MODERN'S WET

            olio's
quite the imbroglio

and the palsy
lights all the ships at sea

let's go

        the submarines over Russia
                are grimy

well, my
fingers thirst

                then an example is the flu
                the new mild form of it

            at any rate I have this idea of the old war

or my behind's itch

though you'd think I can stay where I am

I feel outdone

and that's rich
        it seems you can do too much

A tall cat arches

with its legs together from
the height of its back

       this is the way it goes
       all up and down the snow

  it's out of mind but marches
  the slinging weather
  compounding cracks

  behind everything is confused
  and around it's a bit bruised
  the way everybody's used

      H u n t s

   J i g

under and everybody looks like a fish
the blinding seas off Florida

      the trio's ebb
      or rippling away

        glass bottom swell
       to the floe sky

   and the land upstream, sleep
   from where life is

the milky way
     looks like some ultimate river

  horizons point on a circle

the meadow swirls the island bay

R o l l i n g

to touch
or imagine we touch

       (a stiff cat

my
guts overhead
or underneath

I see

in the dark

I have to feel

what the light was
like

I have to feel

in the light

the blue world
out the air through

roaming

 shells, giraffe

               O   p o s s i b l e

     I had visions of the raids and even a dream once. Getting back
to the chairs and the table. I knew they were porous After the
smash of the ugly cars in the wall   O to turn the time back, now
we have this history to compare.
          Outer soil in the spring. Scraping on the stones, clots, and
the roots. To grow tomatoes And bees   Toads And the
mushrooms by themselves Wild   And how was the advice?
          Putting out the oil in the movie, not too fast. Not in this
country,she had to go around to each separate lamp Other things
ready   on the stained earth when it might be too late already   It
was a bad business. But nothing.   A grip
     The frail planes , them you couldn't see by moments Looked
over the side The lone wolf. Them you couldn't see by moments. He
waved his hand, a grin. Glory jaw under the goggling massk. Dust.
Once you got in the hole you were all right now with the people who
were there from before. The grey clouds coughing white
or white clouds stuttering gray between the house and the hole. It was
safe to have light under the beams. The gloomy roar outside its
reach. Everything went dark. It faded out. The next day a new
airfield. It came through, just like he said you would
     I woke up many times, but couldn't see too many things. The
roads choked with green leaves admitting the light boughs Or
we made the shadows flicker the rain on one side
                              .the gloomy rear.

          Close up

I lie across the bed with my matched feet
        w e   l i v e   i n   t h e   g r e a t   w - o r l d
the ceiling above my eyes just like my toes
It looks like I'm dying but I can't see, what goes on

In the front room a television is playing
The old movies, like we went down the corner as kids
Only these are the grade A's, the classes with affairs and bibs

In the drawing-room they are saying something as the scene opens
A repetition It's just like the first night
I don't know what's hit me, I saw the trails before sunset
  I can't actually tell the placement of stars
  while the beaches of my childhood may still be white

March,

sparrow twittering in the snow
 the empty and the full
window on the fall
the partially bare floor
    is what I like,   under
              my feet the cellar melts

It is near freezing along the ground
the car fusing the dog barks
the phone cries   dying creation

raised trunks   doors
in light houses behind the screens

      the birds holding the air with their crumbs

      streets   the sky over and over again

          wedges and tolling packs of sound

Night. Everything falls flat
The dump of the world. Even within gravity,
the cold. There is a woman
 playing piano   we do not see color
for some space   There were green trees, the country,

 The houses were farminghouses. The phonograph, too
        simple as a road. The ceiling is white
And somewhere now clouds leave the sky

  Look at it, the keyboard's marking time
  inside like a harp something
  breakable, it's as if eternal

  the thing drags out, had to be figured out
  a long time back   she remembers the tones

  in FRance. There will be some years after this
  after last year

                     she wears glasses
  at least in giving a study, patience

      echoes   leaves, distantly
        blocking the window
                          in the broad dark

     at the muffed room

          C l o u d i n g

over by the tree slant roll above the ridgepile where the
sparrows and dark birds flurried below behind
under the empty blue, close on the roof, wings, back and
come forth,ward feet. Motors cut the lawn, how many types
on one property, man's mitts. Sounds like it was far away.
Already the rain, gone, enough of it, irregular, produced
heavily lengthy aisle screenings,interval yesterday. The
clouds shift to a different frame. There are all lines,
which they cross, and open the bays, leaving, shape.
                                              Cats
and dogs, and more,rove.Around the sky is another view.
Boy, the way yesterday, last year, and two years ago,
three years, cutting the grass, energy of heels up forward
a lot of effort and strain. His costly soles fully visi-
ble, on the slope towards the ranch style, going back
both sides of the brick steps to the basement where the
flowerbeds of whatever plants there are like sills. L
pattern a couple of times. He backs up the width of the
lawn, once all the way, both grass and flag stone, the
waste in these days unfathomable a minute, yet soon, any-
way, he turns around. Then, briefly, guiding angular.
It's a rather small front house, at that. The sparrows in
the air, truncate.

            A man comes past with a hard
shine deepily blue boat on two wheels far to the fore of
him, almost wet as it is, holding it by one hand, level
with the wrist, and above that the elbow, and a string.
His duds in there. The greatest morning you can imagine.
How are you going to get it through the woods? So it
should be tremendous evening too. It doesn't go in small
packages. It makes the afternoon odd. Sometimes the rain
lowers here.

          R i n g   i n

                    rather silently, drums
                    and light, weaving on
the abstract forest driving
down in the picture of dark
earth courses itself past
ocean, the times

   not exactly a golden rain
and the stars borne in the distant future

 broken to ages already
    you have thousands of directions
    there is the hot and cold

so the light dies
in the bulb minutes on end
way after 12 the party
     picks up and we
angle ourselves
talking along the wall
     oranges   cookies.

        raining outside
making a scene, somebody came in
ignoring a cold window

I said, it's already half an hour past with
and the calendar by the sink

brand new

and the greyed fat man with the hat on
I can hardly believe it's morning

frost
in appreciative assent.

        the flowers appear on the earth

ROUND MOVIE

the man traveling
thinks nothing of

this, Nothing of what
     all the way

Mountains, a minute, a
 very old thing
       the wet places
just dangerous gracefulness   L o o k i n g   f o r
you see? no, go
left of it   you   S o l o m o n ' s
have been unhurt   (but
                                          M i n e s

    proper cautions
        (there is, if

     some guarantee

 in life

        a good time

unheard of
     (I never heard
  I don't remember it

the hoof's upset
such a land
              break
                  rhythm for
      passing
and the earth
        echo

eventually, eventually
   it may happen
 but that's not an end

      to drink
and the fire
burns itself out
                  (but that is not all
            starting
 it doesn't matter
 after   how
      everything

     unseen   (like anyone

except for those eyes

whose turn is
            immediate, instantaneous

```
frightfully, those beasts
with cries as
they delay
a motion for
                              "blaze
              (not knowing which action

      they exhaust
themselves
  beyond reach

          to proceed somewhere


the straight mountains

            and the hideous men
  marked as where
            (cities might be
      for life
                  their small towns
          different animals
```

```
Waiting to die
waiting,  the moment
waiting to spend

enable us to be thoughtless
enable us to think

            to walk, to fly
              where to lie down

          running,  the water
                  and earth

    get out of your cars

          (the vineyard is the curse
            the green weeds are hard
```

so many things
like running the clock back
                dividing
    the world, separate
                        gears
      ball and bat, time
    we ended up nowhere and went
                without looking

            and yet all the abstraction of it
                    the familiar
      as it turned out not important
      as the unknown, and what mattered
    the speck   as in
          our empty images

                        memory up and down

            waiting to clear away into
          sunshine and more streets
          or the relieving season of storms
              the clock getting it over with
          impregnably in the
            wall,   interwoven
                  the silence out of the wind

          driving through, the tricycle in the way
          of the lumbering trucks, bright models
          cars and the mysterious
          shelved salt, tanks
          easily bared, and the figures
          which weren't toys, skunks
          under the seat, and the possible
          legendary mice, and cats
                            squirrels
            by grandmother's attic, to
                  look back and cast
          nuts, the wise
                against walls

            the boys tossing the daily from farther off

D o   i t   y r s e l f

```
 Now they have two cars to clean
 the front and back lawns
 bloom in the drought

                   why not turn the other radio on the
           pious hopes of the Red Sox

  yes, that's a real gangling kid coming down the street

  he'll grow up

            he'll fill out

          sponges with handles

              we got trinaural hearing

     -they are taller than their cars
```

The Man-Eater

```
 " What gets printed

The trivial things
make the 'fiction',  we seem to have found out.
                     And the news
should be edited

Titles, ideas etc.

compulsive judgments
I write my friends,  ah, neglect of the weather
and the non-existent extent of the man next door

But in fiction I make it up
 what I can do, reducing it all
down like the rain from huge clouds

as if there were never floods
```

253

The amazement of these cripples around me
at a few words,   unable
in my feet and so forth,   ah
truly beautiful voice

                                              for its own sake

t h e   b o a t

g o e s   b a c k
                    for every lightning there is thunder
a n d   f o r t h   I say, when the storm comes up   o!
                         woman lacing the land

                              terrific, somebody says

        say how about the water, is somebody's chip in
                think we might be in a dangerous spot

                              sure,   wonder
                                how can these rods take it

        well, maybe we're caught   but we're movin,too

              the slow sun is winning

cruel and dark, the city
of all men, close

the window, the
streets remain empty

corner around which to blast
or focus, the earth basements

stone bits

a great garage ceiling
the room lights up

blocked like the heavy sign
paint, interior trees
but specialty is the home

a various momentum
the old office windows

          shack   the powerhouse
          weeds
          the station grown with vine

dog's tongue, causeway
cat angle, hardware
retrieving the lost park

store box with the generations
of color girls

   how things have always been eaten

      infinity to wires
       the work, inconceivable

  as it is, each
  one is doing his part

        dolls ragged on the steps

  even the switch is hidden

      it's just as well

the indians had their tents
     and a few plugs or cigars

circle children
reading about it

the hot nights slept on cement

  the sewer curbs

```
THE MURALS OF PICASSO
cities, more walls !  more walls

and go to the slums  the sun beats
             in America


        ((post birds  the world is mine
                 to live with it   ))
```

```
        Mirror

A man and a woman and two big cars
A growing baby, That is Mamma's, that is daddy's
It is summer. a one-car garage

What will they do in the winter
                              they got shoes
   Well, I'll tell you,They'll play cards
 and trade one in

       and a fireplace between the house and garage
 one in the basement and one upstairs

             another baby
      in a few summers, as they say
      3 cars
```

Don Waynor in a Bechuanaland

        you're friendly with the cats
        as I am, more often than you
          I can be friendly too

         this is friendship, not because
        we need each other
        but we are together

        The village idiot was a farce
        like other people the timeless fool
                      in the middle of the wind
                Lear, keeping his tone
          I wonder how many
          have faked that

            I don't know how long you'll be here
        you look like you'll live forever

          File

Let all those memories come flooding back,
What of it we may be blown to the moon next week
All I've done is due to my limitations.

I don't care if big cars come down off the trees
with the clouds going away overhead
It is night and morning, the branches reach for gutters
  it is raining, the hot metal smells   wood

The truth, entirely exact,
is a contradiction
                  the more you can bear
            the more survives

    The clouds slake off,and become
     uninteresting sea

        moment

              the sightless shores, farther

        life goes on in passing

T o   D e p e n d   O n   A n y t h i n g   i s
          t o   C h a n g e   P a r t s

Yourself you don't want
to die now though it's happened
but when it comes to the others
leave it to them

you feel bones in reality
and the stones carelessly lying
                    outside and
             rows in the walls

yet the underground has no room for sights
ramming its own shapes

but much as the future changes it
is the plane circling
the future of where we are
touched in the moment

the way you sit there
which the body itself recollects
is something I'm certain of

                                        1957   # 1 a

          M i n u t e

        old, looking at them
naturally we remember

 way back from
40, from 35
30   life/

is that way
or this is the life

    their continual points
        emphatically to be made
      every day

o good for you

    and the bad thing
    may be the same
    as regards any
    one

```
If you weep, I think that
others might cry
though it is no matter    The rain
is more fruitful
 to the earth breaking
heavy with birds
and leaves we could
not hold    I
     you push
                  and the fog
shadowing tides

     filling the
                  island, farther
out   dampering it down
until the wet congeals
everywhere in the great
arches
                       for which our sight even
becomes too thin, weed
sand and stone, and the tolerant subdued cats
            the sea, the sun


                    arching      beyond
everything there is
    here   and the birds' scream

hunger   or puff
to the silencing light


                and the eyes open
                again, at the
                blind rain


                    in fear and removal

   you cough   and it is
   not the same
```

the mad bus at sunset

autumn and winter wind

The hydrant with barrels
   the poles on a Thursday
 morning

     ends below the sky

The sunshine is odd
Memories familiar

 ity The
 houses with empty souls the

new life

 the fresh bottles, rid of milk,
        not to be seen through
 the wind, stains, streaked dirt

 the birds quicker than the clouds
        or absolute height/flat extreme plane
  hampered by the buildings

facilities for the beach

        stare under the trucks
            the debit of gas burns
            the rain hollow sewers
            where they pour the pipe in

            mists And the trees
            soak the air branches
            low bound in the wintertime

happy habit
Pray for rain, the radio man   Goodbye
then GIANT MACKEREL, buy cadillacs
You, better,
before forgetting we have to
buy our lingerie at the shop

                leave it on

Always some threat of losing the sky
     when thunder, refreshment
   cloud, unequal to planes
unequal to cloud, reflections
the water and deep land
                Halls of a couple of towns

and at night the lid lifts cars
lengthen, gears rock with the glamorous ceilings
but the picture stays put
lights   seen things
  marvelously stable
                like the family romance

garbage going outside
            disappearing

        or the print easing away in the cellar
 bring you back to the dark forgotten
made into flowers,   rank days

but the cellar lies in wait, now
you almost never go down there
or even up   look out   the attic

     where the boards hold you, out of the tree
     and spread,confining you to the present

             imagination or rippling storm

     or swim where you can't have any clothes

  If even you put on wheels or could fly
I wonder what it would be like

        Meat   you can't see the rain
          except in front of the door

     and out on the long roads
     shortly the truck produce

     tail boards

     heat of the metal sun

  Instead of a blank field where the frost comes, beautiful weed

             these women, their pictured houses
                 man a diligent being

        cricket from somewhere you can't see
 the plain, mass escaping in the mind sound

             trees   wind that shakes or crashes
           brick   the cat squinting the country
           seeds, leaves on a few old stones

                 serious animal, the lonely living
          in danger, springing under the sun, other
        summers become lost
                     even in themselves
        though you could try to take on

             single mass

        the houses, wide like a flower
             poured box

     like the once-stained orange crate

     the ceiling plainer
                 hang of the air   261

                cars like waves further off in the night breeze
                  where the windows open, season through the dark
                      distant a minute, flat on the sea

            the birds cove on the wire out to the fishing
            surf by the island tossing repeated grounds
                    sand
              plane of streets   the vast light
            street fragments, shadow of planks,
                                                corners

                  game, or life for the winter

              the island straight on these miles

              the papered rooms on the road back

                            towns light in the evening

        Crown of blades
                      4 off
                  high in the air
                    a straight whirl

                at 3 o'clock
                        sounds like the air-line

                across the bay

                12 hours later
                          it's the sun
                  who would think it could cool off

                    bad time the end
                    of that

                  it's all safely
            clamped down in the night
                frightening and quiet

                  my spine is knotted, really
                                        separate

            the earth enormous from light and dark

                        a nice daily
                                  mind

        F o r   y o u r   q u i e t   l i m b s

Imogen, was he stupid ?

                        It's a
        foolish situation

all these houses around here are stages
  launching

                        drama
            you want that,don't you?

  a mean garment
                    once

        THE FINE LIFE

when you search   the
                  spontaneous thing

objects
        the belief
  shuts the air

  like the whole world, wanting
          to be serious
              but how can we
          in the future

  the parts to the whole

              I saw some sparrows today
              disappear in a slope of dirt
                  below the road

                  the trees were bare like clouds

          that's true we appreciate
                      children
                      the confused harbor

                T h e   A i r
                          harmonie der Welt

when they talk about ideas, music
and instruments, the cars go by

 on wheels
and the " periodic chart of the atoms
against the wall
                          the heavens
     like a wide field

                    quiet

     though thunder come down

                         in the right place

               the battery stops
               dead like some man's
               body which remains

       F l e c h e . .

 cruel arrows gone, the
night closes down,
element, noises
from beyond-the-weather cars
  a mental weight death like space
    with a little communication?
   the clouds level as the earth
   as they travel the world
                         all walls becoming one

     the stars induce days of rain
      and you can forget ice,
     the secrets made by men
     are dropped off like shadows

   outside the trees waver again
                         the cold around your bodies
     it's curious when to die

Something that really happened
there,   the thought of meaning

at the end of history an old book
                    like open casques
black and white facing the sky
      and the serpent
              the vine become a buffed stick

    the names of places and produce and men and acts
          as I used to conceive of the woods
      as a not deathless mass
        or the tracks a necessity

"what this is, I can see his"
    the lack

some nonsense

      while they wouldn't understand

    a gardening of verse
    a history of england

              B o u l e v a r d s ,   t e r r a c e s
                          t o u c h
            THE CONCRETE GLASS

                      vanguard too

staring at the supermarket
    close the eyes, it is still there

  this is the invisible
    added to what there was

                      errors

    the people are walking
    and parking is a waste

      plenty of light and space
        in the night

                    the old rutted ground

Do the dogs know why they bark?
      something they feel   the rain too
              over the familiar houses

But they've stopped. Things always slow

      the cat's habit of sleep on the roof
     at the hole of the bathroom under
     the open skylight

        take it for granted "Invent" the
        cat sleeps on the edge

   and the birds he chases have
   plenty of space

December 57   # 2 b

     T h e   D e a d   d o g

Ah, mutnik,
Kerensky says it's no good
and maybe he knows about it
 better than us all
    is the friend

but someday the grandmothers may grow wise
and speak the calculus

making a fierce language

266

OR FEAR ITSELF

     o l d   s i l v e r y   t o n e s

The gentle voice, whining
    a people

            joy in their moment

      that it was

              some vigor

crippled
         Dear Mamma ..
    coasting
          look at tomorrow
  today   not dangerous

        the unconquerable men, these
    at the table, faith

          B   o   o   m   !

            (the Xmas tree

   a "good education"

    and a "useful job".

   any man

      Mamma, a great lady

         - does not come back

    "for the 7th consecutive time"

    to a worn present

"my little dog resents it"

    on the same side

   you should pardon me when I sit down

Account   of   it   being   Christmas

A lonely corner
      of the orchestra

  in Haydn's Creation
   Paradise lost

  with the Master looking like Dagwood

  and the chorus a german type

  the way they dress

              there are so many worlds

He didn't really want
a knockout he
      knocked him out

  after five years I began
  to miss you the
  buds were about to flower
  again, in the poisonous air

  it was a grub's life
  Sometimes you live to fight again
  the same plastered wall
  against the crickets' green
                              5 0
  the same square. we passed
  mountains, windings, some scouts   G r a n d
  stood on the long road,
  what they grow up to be

   you're always killing yourself

   to sweat   the typewriters, for instance,
  were all right there, to expand
   the prize
  They were all sitting back

       whatever happened was it
   the unknown ache in his face

              a surprise
         finish, for the moment

early 1958   # 4 b

          a   v i r g i n

don't realize what a
fine thing is the ceiling   only
        when I get used to it

    when I go to sleep there's the sky
    lighted
              around the shade

      it takes experience

    that close-fitting night

    shops, for
    the country flourishes
                the street should go on

      and daylight's down on the floor
      as well as the giving earth

    one wall has a reproduction
      of the sea,   and green land

      behind her a rock,
                  but far enough
        to let it through like sound

            and that's the thing that comes back
                  because a sound is soft

        the child on the face of a table

        her right shoulder passed
        before some cloth fold

              egypt,   or Italy

269

BUT

    the theory is practical the
    transformation scene
               is fantastic

    dying is strange

    a great imagination
    to look at the thin-shored cloud
     at the bottom of day

          the unexpected flow

            No conquest but the green isle
      or comfortable city, with patches of wood
      say,   skies without god

       provide sleep

       to rearrange

         a birth

       where the dry trees are grown

   and what would you give? land.
    now you have ruled the depths

clouds complicated as stars
high   in the air

   like mountains,   one in the middle

              the
        evening, because of the sun

     above the swimmers, the beach
     men

           those free relations

        mirror the moon in the west

                  ah, those bird-watchers
           have a new object

                 Boston

                    hills

        the sign of the earth
         after a rain

         colors November

            the road curved

              the road straightened
                that coast lifted off

        another brief shower
        the earth seas

                sound

             history is tall

             clouds   the lost space

             clouds, the moving doors

        the wind breaks on the corner

        the day in the house

A n   o m e n t (A n o n , S i r)

    important and so for
opera

      one thing young

  when you are

   the singer
            's

   imagination

 in time   sound

   and music
     opening images

   or a bursting
  veil   for instance

    romantic breath

     whatever is space

      or paint

T h a t   w a s   b - f l a t

The earth before me, and the sky
                              and you talk
the plunging sleep, echoes of great
                      work, unfinished day

swing the contingent machine
the sun constant a slow
                      depth   small dark

and goes over into a lost moon, ugly animation
  but continues and keeps on

 rising

  shot by explosive pasts

  in brassiness and beauty

  time is complete
  no panorama

        I don't care

                  the tree   the thunder   leaves alone

    and the instrument on the table
    is a useful thing

                      the 9th
                swinging down the street

ah, those cats

        shaking it off

          they're still in the snow

    the garage is closed

    windows in the doors

    a small roof
                    grate, faded back

    while the cats   you think there is

    something to eye

          the chickens were people
          to spring

Goodman, taste
that clarinet, Amadeus ,

the night-long draught

the great mass

THEN

that's time
that moves like a god

In her quiet motorcycle
little car

it's a cinch to drive

The vast illusions
never move off
the miscellaneous movies
                    shack

  the stages are frames
  but limitlessly wide

  look at the park
  something a shipped town
other full periods

        instead of hanging around

  you people hanging around
  the old peanut bar

  and the aisles

  which might be a church
  fanned by factories

  at the end of which a glade

  grownups in the mind

                the tv is too small

The old papers
            in the old mailbox
                        before they're delivered
                        the old houses
            are all right

    the grahndstahnd at
        Wonderlahnd

    pilate's daughter

            we go again around the pylon

      the splendid fuel
        tank up

            inquisitive dog
                        a jumping boy

            flat on the wind
                        ok

            the baby's soon grown

              tenement slice

        the railroad bridge is

        who would think of coating it

      the radio billboard

        which is an ad

            same as the street

WATER-PISTOL

The kids are still
talking of flame-throwers

I wonder about

the guided missile

        maybe it's used by police

c. 1958

Something I won't see
        is the tree deep as the branch
And leaves against the sky

while the cat among the cauliflower
sinks in and out, trying
less of a sight

and even two cats
        I don't know
    the productivity

the man with the limp in back
has suddenly this
                new car
but the cat, familiarly
across the yard

        or else ease in
        the trees, the
        birds who don't climb

fallow roof
and the streets, manifold
as if uphill.

the shadow of the towel three flights up
as the wind moves it
the sun comes out

  nowhere, I can see
 the crow nest

    as if the sparrow talking

planes rattle the teeth
of my home

this month

so many walls
some other blue day
descends into night

the still beach absorbs
searching, a thing that's lost

inland, a number of farms

    any of the seasons

A book has a picture of
a warm landscape

(above the rattling pavement)

beside me the lawn
has been plowed up a little
like the garden it used to be

and the grass is around the tree
            blade as may be for the apples

  leaning, drifting to wastes

 tomorrow
 a keen, swaying rain
 yet to come off

 and how does the sun checker
 or the leaves lie raked

　　　　f u t u r e

open the beyond
underworld exits and entrances
the smoke going up among the stars

shivering ware

in Athens the dust

　　　and elsewhere a pine and
　　oak
　　　　　　　　　dusty olives

　　　in the sea green

　　　　　　　　　　Wind

　　is a strong man

　　ichor is blood
　　　　　　　　　　　　what dies must be born, they said
　　　on the ground

　　　　　　　to drink
　　　　　　memory after

　　　　　　　forgetfulness

　　　raise up the dead he's a
　　machine

　　　　walking so stiffly

　　　　　　both sleeping and awake

　　　in its junction the soul
　　　had memory to go by

other lives

in other streets

you carrots
  rabbits

garage office

it might just as well be
      the temple

but the day is
    temporary

but at night there's the sea

    putting the children to bed
    by the sidewalk
    in the dumb cabined room

all these long cars
legal on the black roads
a more certain speed

here's mercury again

a mile of stone   houses ,

  the sea screens the beach

leaves at the top
                  hill trees

     birds flock

          we'll never remain
                    by the coal lighthouse

  Let's take to our boats
  and crickets' shoes

                all kinds
                protuberating

                    snaky

                series

                    A   b e d o u i n

the water tank
drippings underneath

 camel

the even maze of the desert

rise in a direction

the hills slipping up
 out, off light

   the way it looks
   you might have rain
       one of those months

      no Palestinian cactus

        to reflect a private plane
        out near a good home

      sawdust and butchery .

              shopping

            everything snarls,   the
            toy train

            putting them in for hottop
            putting in to them hottop
            putting in for them a hottop

            models get convenient

            water tent
                        maize
                          a

L'Espagne en coplas

Pour le pauvre sans le sou
Quatre maisons toujours ouvertes
L'hôpital ou la prison
L'eglise ou le cimetière...

De la poussière de la terre
Moi j'arrache les coplas
L'une n'est pas finie
Que j'en tiens une autre.

Regarde ce que dit le proverbe
De ne croire que ce que tu vois
Uniquement!

Qui a raison et qui a tort?
Songe
Que tort en ce monde est mensonge
Il n'est rien de vrai que la mort.

Les femmes comme les bas
C'est pareillement bâti
Si un jour un seul point craque
Tout est rousti!

Même le bois des montagnes
Souffre de partage
Du grande on fait les saints
Du petit le charbon.

Si seul naître une fois
Si seul aimer une fois
Si seul vivre une fois
Si seul mourir une fois!

Partition

For the poor without money
Four houses are always open
The hospital or the prison
The church or the cemetery...

From the dust in the road
I weave you verses
Not one is over
But I take up another.

Look at what the proverb says,
Don't believe all you see
          by itself!

Who is right and who is wrong?
Imagine!
The world is a lie
Nothing is truer than death.

Women like the first stones
Boats and buildings on the same lines
If one thing gives
Everything is wound up!

Even the wood from the mountains
Undergoes treatment,
Either the big saints
Or the small coals.

If it's only to be born once
If it's only to love one time
If it's just to live one time
If it's only to die without noise!

‡ The French is from Espagne, par
   Dominique Aubier et Manuel
   Tuñon de Lara ‡

        B o r o d i n

The steppes of asia last
night about here
in the spring
bloom and they said
it is Music. (rhythm that
crosses lines

passing on
     another time
east, to
join the sun

        or rather the light on
               towards

examine
extrinsics

the fringes involve dividing each
     other, true, even the
     unfinishing flowers

bent so

        and the land cut
        itself